life

APPLICATION® BIBLE STUDIES

Part 1:
Complete text of Romans with study notes and features from the
Life Application Study Bible

Part 2:
Thirteen lessons for individual or group study

Study questions written and edited by

Rev. Ed Trenner
Rev. David R. Veerman
Dr. James C. Galvin
Dr. Bruce B. Barton

New Living Translation®

Tyndale House Publishers, Inc.
Carol Stream, Illinois

romans

Visit Tyndale's exciting Web site at www.tyndale.com

New Living Translation, NLT, the New Living Translation logo, and *Life Application* are registered trademarks of Tyndale House Publishers, Inc.

Life Application Bible Studies: Romans

ISBN 978-1-4143-2563-7

Printed in the United States of America

15 14 13 12 11 10 09
7   6   5   4   3   2   1

CONTENTS

1. **C**ONTEXT

2. **O**BSERVATION

3. **M**EANING

4. **A**PPLICATION

(1.) STYLE OF WRITING -
  - A. LETTER
  - B. POEM
  - C. NARRATIVE
  - D. PROPHETIC

2. WHO WROTE IT, TO WHO, CIRCUMSTANCES
3. WHAT WAS PREVIOUS
4. POLITICAL & SOCIAL SCENE

(2)
- SURPRISES? INTERESTING POINTS?
- KEY WORDS OR PHRASES
- REPEATED WORDS OR IDEAS
- CULTURAL ISSUES
- HOW ARE PEOPLE RELATING TO EACH OTHER AND GOD OR JESUS
- MAIN POINTS OR POINT

(3)
- DOES IT RELATE TO OTHER PARTS OF BIBLE?
- TO JESUS?
- HUMAN NATURE?
- WHAT DOES IT TEACH ABOUT GOD OR JESUS
- WHAT DID IT MEAN FOR THE PEOPLE AT THE TIME

(4).
- HOW DOES THIS CHALLENGE OR CONFIRM WHAT I KNOW?
- IS MY ATTITUDE WRONG?
- SOMETHING I NEED TO CONFESS?
- DOES THIS PASSAGE CALL ME TO CHANGE THE WAY I LIVE
- POINTS TO PRAY ABOUT

A NOTE TO READERS

The *Holy Bible,* New Living Translation, was first published in 1996. It quickly became one of the most popular Bible translations in the English-speaking world. While the NLT's influence was rapidly growing, the Bible Translation Committee determined that an additional investment in scholarly review and text refinement could make it even better. So shortly after its initial publication, the committee began an eight-year process with the purpose of increasing the level of the NLT's precision without sacrificing its easy-to-understand quality. This second-generation text was completed in 2004 and is reflected in this edition of the New Living Translation. An additional update with minor changes was subsequently introduced in 2007.

The goal of any Bible translation is to convey the meaning and content of the ancient Hebrew, Aramaic, and Greek texts as accurately as possible to contemporary readers. The challenge for our translators was to create a text that would communicate as clearly and powerfully to today's readers as the original texts did to readers and listeners in the ancient biblical world. The resulting translation is easy to read and understand, while also accurately communicating the meaning and content of the original biblical texts. The NLT is a general-purpose text especially good for study, devotional reading, and reading aloud in worship services.

We believe that the New Living Translation—which combines the latest biblical scholarship with a clear, dynamic writing style—will communicate God's word powerfully to all who read it. We publish it with the prayer that God will use it to speak his timeless truth to the church and the world in a fresh, new way.

The Publishers
October 2007

INTRODUCTION TO THE
NEW LIVING TRANSLATION

Translation Philosophy and Methodology

English Bible translations tend to be governed by one of two general translation theories. The first theory has been called "formal-equivalence," "literal," or "word-for-word" translation. According to this theory, the translator attempts to render each word of the original language into English and seeks to preserve the original syntax and sentence structure as much as possible in translation. The second theory has been called "dynamic-equivalence," "functional-equivalence," or "thought-for-thought" translation. The goal of this translation theory is to produce in English the closest natural equivalent of the message expressed by the original-language text, both in meaning and in style.

Both of these translation theories have their strengths. A formal-equivalence translation preserves aspects of the original text—including ancient idioms, term consistency, and original-language syntax—that are valuable for scholars and professional study. It allows a reader to trace formal elements of the original-language text through the English translation. A dynamic-equivalence translation, on the other hand, focuses on translating the message of the original-language text. It ensures that the meaning of the text is readily apparent to the contemporary reader. This allows the message to come through with immediacy, without requiring the reader to struggle with foreign idioms and awkward syntax. It also facilitates serious study of the text's message and clarity in both devotional and public reading.

The pure application of either of these translation philosophies would create translations at opposite ends of the translation spectrum. But in reality, all translations contain a mixture of these two philosophies. A purely formal-equivalence translation would be unintelligible in English, and a purely dynamic-equivalence translation would risk being unfaithful to the original. That is why translations shaped by dynamic-equivalence theory are usually quite literal when the original text is relatively clear, and the translations shaped by formal-equivalence theory are sometimes quite dynamic when the original text is obscure.

The translators of the New Living Translation set out to render the message of the original texts of Scripture into clear, contemporary English. As they did so, they kept the concerns of both formal-equivalence and dynamic-equivalence in mind. On the one hand, they translated as simply and literally as possible when that approach yielded an accurate, clear, and natural English text. Many words and phrases were rendered literally and consistently into English, preserving essential literary and rhetorical devices, ancient metaphors, and word choices that give structure to the text and provide echoes of meaning from one passage to the next.

On the other hand, the translators rendered the message more dynamically when the literal rendering was hard to understand, was misleading, or yielded archaic or foreign wording. They clarified difficult metaphors and terms to aid in the reader's understanding. The translators first struggled with the meaning of the words and phrases in the ancient context; then they rendered the message into clear, natural English. Their goal was to be both faithful to the ancient texts and eminently readable. The result is a translation that is both exegetically accurate and idiomatically powerful.

Translation Process and Team

To produce an accurate translation of the Bible into contemporary English, the translation team needed the skills necessary to enter into the thought patterns of the ancient authors and then to render their ideas, connotations, and effects into clear, contemporary English.

To begin this process, qualified biblical scholars were needed to interpret the meaning of the original text and to check it against our base English translation. In order to guard against personal and theological biases, the scholars needed to represent a diverse group of evangelicals who would employ the best exegetical tools. Then to work alongside the scholars, skilled English stylists were needed to shape the text into clear, contemporary English.

With these concerns in mind, the Bible Translation Committee recruited teams of scholars that represented a broad spectrum of denominations, theological perspectives, and backgrounds within the worldwide evangelical community. Each book of the Bible was assigned to three different scholars with proven expertise in the book or group of books to be reviewed. Each of these scholars made a thorough review of a base translation and submitted suggested revisions to the appropriate Senior Translator. The Senior Translator then reviewed and summarized these suggestions and proposed a first-draft revision of the base text. This draft served as the basis for several additional phases of exegetical and stylistic committee review. Then the Bible Translation Committee jointly reviewed and approved every verse of the final translation.

Throughout the translation and editing process, the Senior Translators and their scholar teams were given a chance to review the editing done by the team of stylists. This ensured that exegetical errors would not be introduced late in the process and that the entire Bible Translation Committee was happy with the final result. By choosing a team of qualified scholars and skilled stylists and by setting up a process that allowed their interaction throughout the process, the New Living Translation has been refined to preserve the essential formal elements of the original biblical texts, while also creating a clear, understandable English text.

The New Living Translation was first published in 1996. Shortly after its initial publication, the Bible Translation Committee began a process of further committee review and translation refinement. The purpose of this continued revision was to increase the level of precision without sacrificing the text's easy-to-understand quality. This second-edition text was completed in 2004, and an additional update with minor changes was subsequently introduced in 2007. This printing of the New Living Translation reflects the updated 2007 text.

Written to Be Read Aloud

It is evident in Scripture that the biblical documents were written to be read aloud, often in public worship (see Nehemiah 8; Luke 4:16-20; 1 Timothy 4:13; Revelation 1:3). It is still the case today that more people will hear the Bible read aloud in church than are likely to read it for themselves. Therefore, a new translation must communicate with clarity and power when it is read publicly. Clarity was a primary goal for the NLT translators, not only to facilitate private reading and understanding, but also to ensure that it would be excellent for public reading and make an immediate and powerful impact on any listener.

The Texts behind the New Living Translation

The Old Testament translators used the Masoretic Text of the Hebrew Bible as represented in *Biblia Hebraica Stuttgartensia* (1977), with its extensive system of textual notes; this is an update of Rudolf Kittel's *Biblia Hebraica* (Stuttgart, 1937). The translators also further compared the Dead Sea Scrolls, the Septuagint and other Greek manuscripts, the Samaritan Pentateuch, the Syriac Peshitta, the Latin Vulgate, and any other versions or manuscripts that shed light on the meaning of difficult passages.

The New Testament translators used the two standard editions of the Greek New Testament: the *Greek New Testament,* published by the United Bible Societies (UBS, fourth revised edition, 1993), and *Novum Testamentum Graece,* edited by Nestle and Aland (NA, twenty-seventh edition, 1993). These two editions, which have the same text but differ in punctuation and textual notes, represent, for the most part, the best in modern textual scholarship. However, in cases where strong textual or other scholarly evidence supported the decision, the translators sometimes chose to differ from the UBS and NA Greek texts and followed variant readings found in other ancient witnesses. Significant textual variants of this sort are always noted in the textual notes of the New Living Translation.

Translation Issues

The translators have made a conscious effort to provide a text that can be easily understood by the typical reader of modern English. To this end, we sought to use only vocabulary and language structures in common use today. We avoided using language likely to become quickly dated or that reflects only a narrow subdialect of English, with the goal of making the New Living Translation as broadly useful and timeless as possible.

But our concern for readability goes beyond the concerns of vocabulary and sentence structure. We are also concerned about historical and cultural barriers to understanding the Bible, and we have sought to translate terms shrouded in history and culture in ways that can be immediately understood. To this end:

- We have converted ancient weights and measures (for example, "ephah" [a unit of dry volume] or "cubit" [a unit of length]) to modern English (American) equivalents, since the ancient measures are not generally meaningful to today's readers. Then in the textual footnotes we offer the literal Hebrew, Aramaic, or Greek measures, along with modern metric equivalents.
- Instead of translating ancient currency values literally, we have expressed them in common terms that communicate the message. For example, in the Old Testament, "ten shekels of silver" becomes "ten pieces of silver" to convey the intended message. In the New Testament, we have often translated the "denarius" as "the normal daily wage" to facilitate understanding. Then a footnote offers: "Greek *a denarius*, the payment for a full day's wage." In general, we give a clear English rendering and then state the literal Hebrew, Aramaic, or Greek in a textual footnote.
- Since the names of Hebrew months are unknown to most contemporary readers, and since the Hebrew lunar calendar fluctuates from year to year in relation to the solar calendar used today, we have looked for clear ways to communicate the time of year the Hebrew months (such as Abib) refer to. When an expanded or interpretive rendering is given in the text, a textual note gives the literal rendering. Where it is possible to define a specific ancient date in terms of our modern calendar, we use modern dates in the text. A textual footnote then gives the literal Hebrew date and states the rationale for our rendering. For example, Ezra 6:15 pinpoints the date when the postexilic Temple was completed in Jerusalem: "the third day of the month Adar." This was during the sixth year of King Darius's reign (that is, 515 B.C.). We have translated that date as March 12, with a footnote giving the Hebrew and identifying the year as 515 B.C.
- Since ancient references to the time of day differ from our modern methods of denoting time, we have used renderings that are instantly understandable to the modern reader. Accordingly, we have rendered specific times of day by using approximate equivalents in terms of our common "o'clock" system. On occasion, translations such as "at dawn the next morning" or "as the sun was setting" have been used when the biblical reference is more general.
- When the meaning of a proper name (or a wordplay inherent in a proper name) is relevant to the message of the text, its meaning is often illuminated with a textual footnote. For example, in Exodus 2:10 the text reads: "The princess named him Moses, for she explained, 'I lifted him out of the water.'" The accompanying footnote reads: "*Moses* sounds like a Hebrew term that means 'to lift out.'"

  Sometimes, when the actual meaning of a name is clear, that meaning is included in parentheses within the text itself. For example, the text at Genesis 16:11 reads: "You are to name him Ishmael (*which means 'God hears'*), for the LORD has heard your cry of distress." Since the original hearers and readers would have instantly understood the meaning of the name "Ishmael," we have provided modern readers with the same information so they can experience the text in a similar way.
- Many words and phrases carry a great deal of cultural meaning that was obvious to the original readers but needs explanation in our own culture. For example, the phrase "they beat their breasts" (Luke 23:48) in ancient times meant that people were very upset, often in mourning. In our translation we chose to translate this phrase dynamically for clarity: "They went home *in deep sorrow.*" Then we included a footnote with the literal Greek, which reads: "Greek *went home beating their breasts.*" In other similar cases, however, we have sometimes chosen to illuminate the existing literal expression to make it immediately understandable. For example, here we might have expanded the literal Greek phrase to read: "They went home

beating their breasts *in sorrow.*" If we had done this, we would not have included a textual footnote, since the literal Greek clearly appears in translation.

- Metaphorical language is sometimes difficult for contemporary readers to understand, so at times we have chosen to translate or illuminate the meaning of a metaphor. For example, the ancient poet writes, "Your neck is *like* the tower of David" (Song of Songs 4:4). We have rendered it "Your neck is *as beautiful as* the tower of David" to clarify the intended positive meaning of the simile. Another example comes in Ecclesiastes 12:3, which can be literally rendered: "Remember him . . . when the grinding women cease because they are few, and the women who look through the windows see dimly." We have rendered it: "Remember him before your teeth—your few remaining servants—stop grinding; and before your eyes—the women looking through the windows—see dimly." We clarified such metaphors only when we believed a typical reader might be confused by the literal text.

- When the content of the original language text is poetic in character, we have rendered it in English poetic form. We sought to break lines in ways that clarify and highlight the relationships between phrases of the text. Hebrew poetry often uses parallelism, a literary form where a second phrase (or in some instances a third or fourth) echoes the initial phrase in some way. In Hebrew parallelism, the subsequent parallel phrases continue, while also furthering and sharpening, the thought expressed in the initial line or phrase. Whenever possible, we sought to represent these parallel phrases in natural poetic English.

- The Greek term *hoi Ioudaioi* is literally translated "the Jews" in many English translations. In the Gospel of John, however, this term doesn't always refer to the Jewish people generally. In some contexts, it refers more particularly to the Jewish religious leaders. We have attempted to capture the meaning in these different contexts by using terms such as "the people" (with a footnote: Greek *the Jewish people*) or "the religious leaders," where appropriate.

- One challenge we faced was how to translate accurately the ancient biblical text that was originally written in a context where male-oriented terms were used to refer to humanity generally. We needed to respect the nature of the ancient context while also trying to make the translation clear to a modern audience that tends to read male-oriented language as applying only to males. Often the original text, though using masculine nouns and pronouns, clearly intends that the message be applied to both men and women. A typical example is found in the New Testament letters, where the believers are called "brothers" (*adelphoi*). Yet it is clear from the content of these letters that they were addressed to all the believers—male and female. Thus, we have usually translated this Greek word as "brothers and sisters" in order to represent the historical situation more accurately.

  We have also been sensitive to passages where the text applies generally to human beings or to the human condition. In some instances we have used plural pronouns (they, them) in place of the masculine singular (he, him). For example, a traditional rendering of Proverbs 22:6 is: "Train up a child in the way he should go, and when he is old he will not turn from it." We have rendered it: "Direct your children onto the right path, and when they are older, they will not leave it." At times, we have also replaced third person pronouns with the second person to ensure clarity. A traditional rendering of Proverbs 26:27 is: "He who digs a pit will fall into it, and he who rolls a stone, it will come back on him." We have rendered it: "If you set a trap for others, you will get caught in it yourself. If you roll a boulder down on others, it will crush you instead."

  We should emphasize, however, that all masculine nouns and pronouns used to represent God (for example, "Father") have been maintained without exception. All decisions of this kind have been driven by the concern to reflect accurately the intended meaning of the original texts of Scripture.

Lexical Consistency in Terminology
For the sake of clarity, we have translated certain original-language terms consistently, especially within synoptic passages and for commonly repeated rhetorical phrases, and within

certain word categories such as divine names and non-theological technical terminology (e.g., liturgical, legal, cultural, zoological, and botanical terms). For theological terms, we have allowed a greater semantic range of acceptable English words or phrases for a single Hebrew or Greek word. We have avoided some theological terms that are not readily understood by many modern readers. For example, we avoided using words such as "justification" and "sanctification," which are carryovers from Latin translations. In place of these words, we have provided renderings such as "made right with God" and "made holy."

The Spelling of Proper Names

Many individuals in the Bible, especially the Old Testament, are known by more than one name (e.g., Uzziah/Azariah). For the sake of clarity, we have tried to use a single spelling for any one individual, footnoting the literal spelling whenever we differ from it. This is especially helpful in delineating the kings of Israel and Judah. King Joash/Jehoash of Israel has been consistently called Jehoash, while King Joash/Jehoash of Judah is called Joash. A similar distinction has been used to distinguish between Joram/Jehoram of Israel and Joram/Jehoram of Judah. All such decisions were made with the goal of clarifying the text for the reader. When the ancient biblical writers clearly had a theological purpose in their choice of a variant name (e.g., Esh-baal/Ishbosheth), the different names have been maintained with an explanatory footnote.

For the names Jacob and Israel, which are used interchangeably for both the individual patriarch and the nation, we generally render it "Israel" when it refers to the nation and "Jacob" when it refers to the individual. When our rendering of the name differs from the underlying Hebrew text, we provide a textual footnote, which includes this explanation: "The names 'Jacob' and 'Israel' are often interchanged throughout the Old Testament, referring sometimes to the individual patriarch and sometimes to the nation."

The Rendering of Divine Names

All appearances of *'el, 'elohim,* or *'eloah* have been translated "God," except where the context demands the translation "god(s)." We have generally rendered the tetragrammaton (*YHWH*) consistently as "the LORD," utilizing a form with small capitals that is common among English translations. This will distinguish it from the name *'adonai,* which we render "Lord." When *'adonai* and *YHWH* appear together, we have rendered it "Sovereign LORD." This also distinguishes *'adonai YHWH* from cases where *YHWH* appears with *'elohim,* which is rendered "LORD God." When *YH* (the short form of *YHWH*) and *YHWH* appear together, we have rendered it "LORD GOD." When *YHWH* appears with the term *tseba'oth,* we have rendered it "LORD of Heaven's Armies" to translate the meaning of the name. In a few cases, we have utilized the transliteration, *Yahweh,* when the personal character of the name is being invoked in contrast to another divine name or the name of some other god (for example, see Exodus 3:15; 6:2-3).

In the New Testament, the Greek word *christos* has been translated as "Messiah" when the context assumes a Jewish audience. When a Gentile audience can be assumed, *christos* has been translated as "Christ." The Greek word *kurios* is consistently translated "Lord," except that it is translated "LORD" wherever the New Testament text explicitly quotes from the Old Testament, and the text there has it in small capitals.

Textual Footnotes

The New Living Translation provides several kinds of textual footnotes, all designated in the text with an asterisk:

- When for the sake of clarity the NLT renders a difficult or potentially confusing phrase dynamically, we generally give the literal rendering in a textual footnote. This allows the reader to see the literal source of our dynamic rendering and how our translation relates to other more literal translations. These notes are prefaced with "Hebrew," "Aramaic," or "Greek," identifying the language of the underlying source text. For example, in Acts 2:42 we translated the literal "breaking of bread" (from the Greek) as "the Lord's Supper" to clarify that this verse refers to the ceremonial practice of the church rather than just an ordinary meal. Then we attached a footnote to "the Lord's Supper," which reads: "Greek *the breaking of bread.*"

- Textual footnotes are also used to show alternative renderings, prefaced with the word "Or." These normally occur for passages where an aspect of the meaning is debated. On occasion, we also provide notes on words or phrases that represent a departure from long-standing tradition. These notes are prefaced with "Tradition-ally rendered." For example, the footnote to the translation "serious skin disease" at Leviticus 13:2 says: "Traditionally rendered *leprosy.* The Hebrew word used throughout this passage is used to describe various skin diseases."
- When our translators follow a textual variant that differs significantly from our stan-dard Hebrew or Greek texts (listed earlier), we document that difference with a foot-note. We also footnote cases when the NLT excludes a passage that is included in the Greek text known as the *Textus Receptus* (and familiar to readers through its transla-tion in the King James Version). In such cases, we offer a translation of the excluded text in a footnote, even though it is generally recognized as a later addition to the Greek text and not part of the original Greek New Testament.
- All Old Testament passages that are quoted in the New Testament are identified by a textual footnote at the New Testament location. When the New Testament clearly quotes from the Greek translation of the Old Testament, and when it differs signifi-cantly in wording from the Hebrew text, we also place a textual footnote at the Old Testament location. This note includes a rendering of the Greek version, along with a cross-reference to the New Testament passage(s) where it is cited (for example, see notes on Proverbs 3:12; Psalms 8:2; 53:3).
- Some textual footnotes provide cultural and historical information on places, things, and people in the Bible that are probably obscure to modern readers. Such notes should aid the reader in understanding the message of the text. For example, in Acts 12:1, "King Herod" is named in this translation as "King Herod Agrippa" and is iden-tified in a footnote as being "the nephew of Herod Antipas and a grandson of Herod the Great."
- When the meaning of a proper name (or a wordplay inherent in a proper name) is relevant to the meaning of the text, it is either illuminated with a textual footnote or included within parentheses in the text itself. For example, the footnote concerning the name "Eve" at Genesis 3:20 reads: "*Eve* sounds like a Hebrew term that means 'to give life.' " This wordplay in the Hebrew illuminates the meaning of the text, which goes on to say that Eve "would be the mother of all who live."

AS WE SUBMIT this translation for publication, we recognize that any translation of the Scrip-tures is subject to limitations and imperfections. Anyone who has attempted to communi-cate the richness of God's Word into another language will realize it is impossible to make a perfect translation. Recognizing these limitations, we sought God's guidance and wisdom throughout this project. Now we pray that he will accept our efforts and use this translation for the benefit of the church and of all people.

We pray that the New Living Translation will overcome some of the barriers of history, cul-ture, and language that have kept people from reading and understanding God's Word. We hope that readers unfamiliar with the Bible will find the words clear and easy to understand and that readers well versed in the Scriptures will gain a fresh perspective. We pray that readers will gain insight and wisdom for living, but most of all that they will meet the God of the Bible and be forever changed by knowing him.

The Bible Translation Committee
October 2007

WHY THE
LIFE APPLICATION STUDY BIBLE
IS UNIQUE

Have you ever opened your Bible and asked the following:

- What does this passage really mean?
- How does it apply to my life?
- Why does some of the Bible seem irrelevant?
- What do these ancient cultures have to do with today?
- I love God; why can't I understand what he is saying to me through his word?
- What's going on in the lives of these Bible people?

Many Christians do not read the Bible regularly. Why? Because in the pressures of daily living they cannot find a connection between the timeless principles of Scripture and the ever-present problems of day-by-day living.

God urges us to apply his word (Isaiah 42:23; 1 Corinthians 10:11; 2 Thessalonians 3:4), but too often we stop at accumulating Bible knowledge. This is why the *Life Application Study Bible* was developed—to show how to put into practice what we have learned.

Applying God's word is a vital part of one's relationship with God; it is the evidence that we are obeying him. The difficulty in applying the Bible is not with the Bible itself, but with the reader's inability to bridge the gap between the past and present, the conceptual and practical. When we don't or can't do this, spiritual dryness, shallowness, and indifference are the results.

The words of Scripture itself cry out to us, "But don't just listen to God's word. You must do what it says. Otherwise, you are only fooling yourselves" (James 1:22). The *Life Application Study Bible* helps us to obey God's word. Developed by an interdenominational team of pastors, scholars, family counselors, and a national organization dedicated to promoting God's word and spreading the gospel, the *Life Application Study Bible* took many years to complete. All the work was reviewed by several renowned theologians under the directorship of Dr. Kenneth Kantzer.

The *Life Application Study Bible* does what a good resource Bible should: It helps you understand the context of a passage, gives important background and historical information, explains difficult words and phrases, and helps you see the interrelationship of Scripture. But it does much more. The *Life Application Study Bible* goes deeper into God's word, helping you discover the timeless truth being communicated, see the relevance for your life, and make a personal application. While some study Bibles attempt application, over 75 percent of this Bible is application oriented. The notes answer the questions "So what?" and "What does this passage mean to me, my family, my friends, my job, my neighborhood, my church, my country?"

Imagine reading a familiar passage of Scripture and gaining fresh insight, as if it were the first time you had ever read it. How much richer your life would be if you left each Bible reading with a new perspective and a small change for the better. A small change every day adds up to a changed life—and that is the very purpose of Scripture.

WHAT IS APPLICATION?

The best way to define application is to first determine what it is *not*. Application is *not* just accumulating knowledge. Accumulating knowledge helps us discover and understand facts and concepts, but it stops there. History is filled with philosophers who knew what the Bible said but failed to apply it to their lives, keeping them from believing and changing. Many think that understanding is the end goal of Bible study, but it is really only the beginning.

Application is *not* just illustration. Illustration only tells us how someone else handled a similar situation. While we may empathize with that person, we still have little direction for our personal situation.

Application is *not* just making a passage "relevant." Making the Bible relevant only helps us to see that the same lessons that were true in Bible times are true today; it does not show us how to apply them to the problems and pressures of our individual lives.

What, then, is application? Application begins by knowing and understanding God's word and its timeless truths. *But you cannot stop there.* If you do, God's word may not change your life, and it may become dull, difficult, tedious, and tiring. A good application focuses the truth of God's word, shows the reader what to do about what is being read, and motivates the reader to respond to what God is teaching. All three are essential to application.

Application is putting into practice what we already know (see Mark 4:24 and Hebrews 5:14) and answering the question "So what?" by confronting us with the right questions and motivating us to take action (see 1 John 2:5-6 and James 2:26). Application is deeply personal—unique for each individual. It makes a relevant truth a personal truth and involves developing a strategy and action plan to live your life in harmony with the Bible. It is the biblical "how to" of life.

You may ask, "How can your application notes be relevant to my life?" Each application note has three parts: (1) an *explanation*, which ties the note directly to the Scripture passage and sets up the truth that is being taught; (2) the *bridge*, which explains the timeless truth and makes it relevant for today; (3) the *application*, which shows you how to take the timeless truth and apply it to your personal situation. No note, by itself, can apply Scripture directly to your life. It can only teach, direct, lead, guide, inspire, recommend, and urge. It can give you the resources and direction you need to apply the Bible; but only you can take these resources and put them into practice.

A good note, therefore should not only give you knowledge and understanding but point you to application. Before you buy any kind of resource study Bible, you should evaluate the notes and ask the following questions: (1) Does the note contain enough information to help me understand the point of the Scripture passage? (2) Does the note assume I know more than I do? (3) Does the note avoid denominational bias? (4) Do the notes touch most of life's experiences? (5) Does the note help me apply God's word?

FEATURES OF THE
LIFE APPLICATION STUDY BIBLE

NOTES
In addition to providing the reader with many application notes, the *Life Application Study Bible* also offers several kinds of explanatory notes, which help the reader understand culture, history, context, difficult-to-understand passages, background, places, theological concepts, and the relationship of various passages in Scripture to other passages.

BOOK INTRODUCTIONS
Each book introduction is divided into several easy-to-find parts:

Timeline. A guide that puts the Bible book into its historical setting. It lists the key events and the dates when they occurred.

Vital Statistics. A list of straight facts about the book—those pieces of information you need to know at a glance.

Overview. A summary of the book with general lessons and applications that can be learned from the book as a whole.

Blueprint. The outline of the book. It is printed in easy-to-understand language and is designed for easy memorization. To the right of each main heading is a key lesson that is taught in that particular section.

Megathemes. A section that gives the main themes of the Bible book, explains their significance, and then tells you why they are still important for us today.

Map. If included, this shows the key places found in that book and retells the story of the book from a geographical point of view.

OUTLINE
The *Life Application Study Bible* has a new, custom-made outline that was designed specifically from an application point of view. Several unique features should be noted:

1. To avoid confusion and to aid memory work, the book outline has only three levels for headings. Main outline heads are marked with a capital letter. Subheads are marked by a number. Minor explanatory heads have no letter or number.

2. Each main outline head marked by a letter also has a brief paragraph below it summarizing the Bible text and offering a general application.

3. Parallel passages are listed where they apply.

PERSONALITY PROFILES
Among the unique features of this Bible are the profiles of key Bible people, including their strengths and weaknesses, greatest accomplishments and mistakes, and key lessons from their lives.

MAPS

The *Life Application Study Bible* has a thorough and comprehensive Bible atlas built right into the book. There are two kinds of maps: a book-introduction map, telling the story of the book, and thumbnail maps in the notes, plotting most geographic movements.

CHARTS AND DIAGRAMS

Many charts and diagrams are included to help the reader better visualize difficult concepts or relationships. Most charts not only present the needed information but show the significance of the information as well.

CROSS-REFERENCES

An updated, exhaustive cross-reference system in the margins of the Bible text helps the reader find related passages quickly.

TEXTUAL NOTES

Directly related to the text of the New Living Translation, the textual notes provide explanations on certain wording in the translation, alternate translations, and information about readings in the ancient manuscripts.

HIGHLIGHTED NOTES

In each Bible study lesson, you will be asked to read specific notes as part of your preparation. These notes have each been highlighted by a bullet (•) so that you can find them easily.

ROMANS

OUR NEED FOR SALVATION
GOD'S GRACE & OUR FAITH
SCOPE OF SALVATION
CHRISTIAN SERVICE

ROMANS

VITAL STATISTICS

PURPOSE:
To introduce Paul to the Romans and to give a sample of his message before he arrives in Rome

AUTHOR:
Paul

ORIGINAL AUDIENCE:
The Christians in Rome

DATE WRITTEN:
About A.D. 57, from Corinth, as Paul was preparing for his visit to Jerusalem.

SETTING:
Apparently Paul had finished his work in the east, and he planned to visit Rome on his way to Spain after first bringing a collection to Jerusalem for the poor Christians there (15:23–28). The Roman church was mostly Jewish but also contained a great number of Gentiles.

KEY VERSE:
"Therefore, since we have been made right in God's sight by faith, we have peace with God because of what Jesus Christ our Lord has done for us" (5:1).

KEY PEOPLE:
Paul, Phoebe

KEY PLACE:
Rome

SPECIAL FEATURES:
Paul wrote Romans as an organized and carefully presented statement of his faith—it does not have the form of a typical letter. He does, however, spend considerable time greeting people in Rome at the end of the letter.

KNOWLEDGEABLE and experienced, the district attorney makes his case. Calling key witnesses to the stand, he presents the evidence. After discrediting the testimonies of witnesses for the defense by skillfully cross-examining them, he concludes with an airtight summary and stirring challenge for the jury. The announced verdict is no surprise. "Guilty" states the foreman, and justice is served.

The apostle Paul was intelligent, articulate, and committed to his calling. Like a skilled lawyer, he presented the case for the gospel clearly and forthrightly in his letter to the believers in Rome.

Paul had heard of the church at Rome, but he had not yet been there, nor had any of the other apostles. Evidently the church had been started by Jews who had come to faith during Pentecost (Acts 2). They had spread the gospel on their return to Rome, and the church had grown.

Although many barriers separated them, Paul felt a bond with these believers in Rome. They were his brothers and sisters in Christ, and he longed to see them face to face. He had never met most of the believers there, yet he loved them. He sent this letter to introduce himself and to make a clear declaration of the faith.

After a brief introduction, Paul presents the facts of the gospel (1:3) and declares his allegiance to it (1:16, 17). He continues by building an airtight case for the lostness of humanity and the necessity for God's intervention (1:18—3:20).

Then Paul presents the Good News: Salvation is available to all, regardless of a person's identity, sin, or heritage. We are saved by *grace* (unearned, undeserved favor from God) through *faith* (complete trust) in Christ and his finished work. Through him we can stand before God justified, "not guilty" (3:21—5:21). With this foundation Paul moves directly into a discussion of the freedom that comes from being saved—freedom from the power of sin (6:1–23), freedom from the domination of the law (7:1–25), freedom to become like Christ and discover God's limitless love (8:1–39).

Speaking directly to his Jewish brothers and sisters, Paul shares his concern for them and explains how they fit into God's plan (9:1—11:12). God has made the way for Jews and Gentiles to be united in the body of Christ; both groups can praise God for his wisdom and love (11:13–36).

Paul explains what it means to live in complete submission to Christ: Use spiritual gifts to serve others (12:3–8), genuinely love others (12:9–21), and be good citizens (13:1–14). Freedom must be guided by love as we build each other up in the faith, being sensitive and helpful to those who are weak (14:1—15:4). Paul stresses unity, especially between Gentiles and Jews (15:5–13). He concludes by reviewing his reasons for writing, outlining his personal plans (15:22–33), greeting his friends, and giving a few final thoughts and greetings from his traveling companions (16:1–27).

As you read Romans, reexamine your commitment to Christ, and reconfirm your relationships with other believers in Christ's body.

THE BLUEPRINT

A. WHAT TO BELIEVE
    (1:1—11:36)
    1. Sinfulness of humanity
    2. Forgiveness of sin through Christ
    3. Freedom from sin's grasp
    4. Israel's past, present, and future

Paul clearly sets forth the foundations of the Christian faith. All people are sinful; Christ died to forgive sin; we are made right with God through faith; this begins a new life with a new relationship with God. Like a sports team that constantly reviews the basics, we will be greatly helped in our faith by keeping close to these foundations. If we study Romans carefully, we will never be at a loss to know what to believe.

B. HOW TO BEHAVE
    (12:1—16:27)
    1. Personal responsibility
    2. Personal notes

Paul gives clear, practical guidelines for the believers in Rome. The Christian life is not abstract theology unconnected with life, but it has practical implications that will affect how we choose to behave each day. It is not enough merely to know the gospel; we must let it transform our life and let God impact every aspect of our lives.

MEGATHEMES

THEME	EXPLANATION	IMPORTANCE
Sin	Sin means refusing to do God's will and failing to do all that God wants. Since Adam's rebellion against God, our nature is to disobey him. Our sin cuts us off from God. Sin causes us to want to live our own way rather than God's way. Because God is morally perfect, just, and fair, he is right to condemn sin.	Each person has sinned, either by rebelling against God or by ignoring his will. No matter what our background or how hard we try to live good and moral lives, we cannot earn salvation or remove our sin. Only Christ can save us.
Salvation	Our sin points out our need to be forgiven and cleansed. Although we don't deserve it, God, in his kindness, reached out to love and forgive us. He provides the way for us to be saved. Christ's death paid the penalty for our sin.	It is good news that God saves us from our sin. But in order to enter into a wonderful new relationship with God, we must believe that Jesus died for us and that he forgives all our sin.
Growth	By God's power, believers are sanctified—made holy. This means we are set apart from sin, enabled to obey and to become more like Christ. When we are growing in our relationship with Christ, the Holy Spirit frees us from the demands of the law and from fear of judgment.	Because we are free from sin's control, the law's demands, and fear of God's punishment, we can grow in our relationship with Christ. By trusting in the Holy Spirit and allowing him to help us, we can overcome sin and temptation.
Sovereignty	God oversees and cares about his people—past, present, and future. God's ways of dealing with people are always fair. Because God is in charge of all creation, he can save whomever he wills.	Because of God's mercy, both Jews and Gentiles can be saved. We all must respond to his mercy and accept his gracious offer of forgiveness. Because he is sovereign, let him reign in your heart.
Service	When our purpose is to give credit to God for his love, power, and perfection in all we do, we can serve him properly. Serving him unifies all believers and enables them to show love and sensitivity to others.	None of us can be fully Christlike by ourselves—it takes the entire body of Christ to fully express Christ. By actively and vigorously building up other believers, Christians can be a symphony of service to God.

A. WHAT TO BELIEVE (1:1—11:36)

Paul begins his message to the Romans by vividly portraying the sinfulness of all people, explaining how forgiveness is available through faith in Christ, and showing what believers experience in life through their new faith. In this section, we learn of the centrality of faith to becoming a Christian and to living the Christian life. Apart from faith, we have no hope in life.

1. Sinfulness of humanity

Greetings from Paul

1 This letter is from Paul, a slave of Christ Jesus, chosen by God to be an apostle and sent out to preach his Good News. ²God promised this Good News long ago through his prophets in the holy Scriptures. ³The Good News is about his Son. In his earthly life he was born into King David's family line, ⁴and he was shown to be* the Son of God when he was raised from the dead by the power of the Holy Spirit.* He is Jesus Christ our Lord. ⁵Through Christ, God has given us the privilege* and authority as apostles to tell Gentiles everywhere what God has done for them, so that they will believe and obey him, bringing glory to his name.

⁶And you are included among those Gentiles who have been called to belong to Jesus Christ. ⁷I am writing to all of you in Rome who are loved by God and are called to be his own holy people.

May God our Father and the Lord Jesus Christ give you grace and peace.

1:3
Matt 1:1; 22:42
Rom 9:5
2 Tim 2:8

1:4
Acts 13:33
Rom 8:11

1:5
Acts 9:15
Rom 16:26
Gal 1:16
Eph 3:8-9

1:7
1 Cor 1:2
2 Cor 1:1
Gal 1:3
Eph 1:1

1:4a Or *and was designated.* **1:4b** Or *by the Spirit of holiness;* or *in the new realm of the Spirit.* **1:5** Or *the grace.*

• **1:1** Paul wrote this letter to the church in Rome. Neither he nor the other church leaders, James and Peter, had yet been to Rome. Most likely, the Roman church had been established by believers who had been at Jerusalem for Pentecost (Acts 2:10) and by travelers who had heard the Good News in other places and had brought it back to Rome (for example, Priscilla and Aquila, Acts 18:2; Romans 16:3-5). Paul wrote the letter to the Romans during his ministry in Corinth (at the end of his third missionary journey just before returning to Jerusalem—Acts 20:3; Romans 15:25) to encourage the believers and to express his desire to visit them someday (within three years he would). The Roman church had no New Testament because the Gospels were not yet being circulated in their final written form. Thus, this letter may well have been the first piece of Christian literature the Roman believers had seen. Written to both Jewish and Gentile Christians, the letter to the Romans is a systematic presentation of the Christian faith.

1:1 When Paul, a devout Jew who had at first persecuted the Christians, became a believer, God used him to spread the Good News throughout the world. Although he was a prisoner, Paul did eventually preach in Rome (Acts 28), perhaps even to Caesar himself. Paul's Profile is found in Acts 9, p. 1837.

• **1:1** Paul humbly calls himself a slave of Christ Jesus and an apostle ("one who is sent"). For a Roman citizen—which Paul was—to choose to be a slave was unthinkable. But Paul chose to be completely dependent on and obedient to his beloved Master. What is your attitude toward Christ, your Master? Our willingness to serve and obey Jesus Christ enables us to be useful and usable servants to do work for him—work that really matters. Obedience begins as we renounce other masters, identify ourselves with Jesus, discover his will and live according to it, and consciously turn away from conflicting interests, even if these interests have been important to us in the past.

1:2 Some of the prophecies predicting the Good News regarding Jesus Christ are found in Genesis 12:3; Psalms 16:10; 40:6-10; 118:22; Isaiah 11:1ff; Zechariah 9:9-11; 12:10; Malachi 4:1-6.

1:3, 4 Paul states that Jesus is the Son of God, the promised Messiah, and the resurrected Lord. Paul calls Jesus a descendant of King David to emphasize that Jesus truly had fulfilled the Old Testament Scriptures predicting that the Messiah would come from David's line. With this statement of faith, Paul declares his agreement with the teaching of all Scripture and of the apostles.

• **1:3-5** Here Paul summarizes the Good News about Jesus Christ, who (1) came as a human by natural descent, (2) was part of the Jewish royal line through David, (3) died and was raised from the

dead, and (4) opened the door for God's grace and kindness to be poured out on us. The book of Romans is an expansion of these themes.

• **1:5** Christians have both a privilege and a great responsibility. Paul and the apostles received the privilege of being called, but they also received the authority and the responsibility to share with others what God has done. God also graciously forgives our sins when we believe in him as Lord. In doing this, we are committing ourselves to begin a new life. Paul's new life also involved a God-given responsibility: to witness about God's Good News to the world as a missionary. God may or may not call you to be a foreign missionary, but he does call you (and all believers) to be Christ's ambassador and to witness to the changed life that Jesus Christ has begun in you.

1:6 Jews and Christians alike stood against the idolatrous Roman religions, and Roman officials often confused the two groups. This was especially easy to do since the Christian church in Rome could have been originally composed of Jewish converts who had attended Pentecost in Jerusalem (see Acts 2:1ff). By the time Paul wrote this letter to the Romans, however, many Gentiles had joined the church. The Jews and the Gentiles needed to know the relationship between Judaism and Christianity.

• **1:6, 7** Paul says that those who become Christians are invited by Jesus Christ to (1) belong to God's family, and (2) be his very own people. What a wonderful expression of what it means to be a Christian! In being reborn into God's family we have the greatest experience of love and the greatest inheritance. Because of all that God has done for us, we strive to be his holy people.

• **1:7** Rome was the capital of the Roman Empire that had spread over most of Europe, North Africa, and the Near East. In New Testament times, Rome was experiencing a golden age. The city was wealthy, literary, and artistic. It was a cultural center, but it was also morally decadent. The Romans worshiped many pagan gods, and even some of the emperors were worshiped. In stark contrast to the Romans, the followers of Christ believed in only one God and lived by his high moral standards.

Christianity was also at odds with the Romans' dependence on military strength. Many Romans were naively pragmatic, believing that any means to accomplish the intended task was good. And for them, nothing worked better than physical might. The Romans trusted in their strong military power to protect them against all enemies. Christians in every age need to be reminded that God is the only permanent source of our security and salvation, and at the same time he is "our Father"!

God's Good News

1:8
Rom 16:19
1 Thes 1:8

1:9
Eph 1:16
Phil 1:8-9
1 Thes 2:5
2 Tim 1:3

1:10
Rom 15:23, 32

1:11
Rom 15:23

1:13
John 15:16
Rom 15:22

⁸Let me say first that I thank my God through Jesus Christ for all of you, because your faith in him is being talked about all over the world. ⁹God knows how often I pray for you. Day and night I bring you and your needs in prayer to God, whom I serve with all my heart* by spreading the Good News about his Son.

¹⁰One of the things I always pray for is the opportunity, God willing, to come at last to see you. ¹¹For I long to visit you so I can bring you some spiritual gift that will help you grow strong in the Lord. ¹²When we get together, I want to encourage you in your faith, but I also want to be encouraged by yours.

¹³I want you to know, dear brothers and sisters,* that I planned many times to visit you, but I was prevented until now. I want to work among you and see spiritual fruit, just as I have

1:9 Or *in my spirit.*   **1:13** Greek *brothers.*

THE GOSPEL GOES TO ROME
When Paul wrote his letter to the church in Rome, he had not yet been there, but he had taken the gospel "from Jerusalem all the way to Illyricum" (15:19). He planned to visit and preach in Rome one day and hoped to continue to take the gospel farther west— even to Spain.

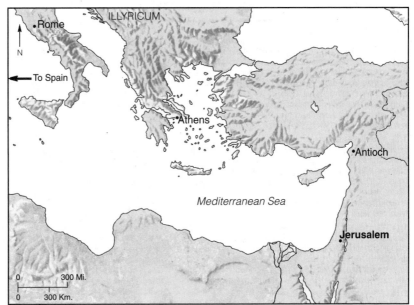

1:8 Paul uses the phrase "I thank my God through Jesus Christ" to emphasize the point that Christ is the one and only mediator between us and God. Through Christ, God sends his love and forgiveness to us; through Christ, we send our thanks to God (see 1 Timothy 2:5).

• **1:8** The Roman Christians, at the Western world's political power center, were highly visible. Fortunately, their reputation was excellent; their strong faith was making itself known around the world. When people talk about your congregation or your denomination, what do they say? Are their comments accurate? Would you rather they noticed other features? What is the best way to get the public to recognize your faith?

• **1:9, 10** When you pray continually about a concern, don't be surprised at how God answers. Paul prayed to visit Rome so he could teach the Christians there. When he finally arrived in Rome, it was as a prisoner (see Acts 28:16). Paul prayed for a safe trip, and he did arrive safely—after getting arrested, slapped in the face, shipwrecked, and bitten by a poisonous snake. When we sincerely pray, God will answer—although in his timing and sometimes in ways we do not expect.

• **1:11-13** A reading of the first few verses of Romans relates Paul's ardent desire to visit Rome and the sovereign hand of God

that had prevented him from getting there for quite some time. The combination of these two factors—Paul's impassioned desire to go to Rome and God's sovereign "no"—resulted in his sitting down to write this letter to the Romans. This letter is a powerful exposition of the Christian faith and has helped countless millions of believers across the centuries since Paul first penned it to the group of believers in Rome. Perhaps there are some "no's" in our lives that God is planning to use greatly if we would just faithfully do what lies directly ahead of us instead of worrying about why we didn't get our way.

1:13 By the end of his third missionary journey, Paul had traveled through Syria, Galatia, Asia, Macedonia, and Achaia. The churches in these areas were made up mostly of Gentile believers.

seen among other Gentiles. ¹⁴For I have a great sense of obligation to people in both the civilized world and the rest of the world,* to the educated and uneducated alike. ¹⁵So I am eager to come to you in Rome, too, to preach the Good News.

¹⁶For I am not ashamed of this Good News about Christ. It is the power of God at work, saving everyone who believes—the Jew first and also the Gentile.* ¹⁷This Good News tells us how God makes us right in his sight. This is accomplished from start to finish by faith. As the Scriptures say, "It is through faith that a righteous person has life."*

God's Anger at Sin

¹⁸But God shows his anger from heaven against all sinful, wicked people who suppress the truth by their wickedness.* ¹⁹They know the truth about God because he has made it obvious to them. ²⁰For ever since the world was created, people have seen the earth and sky. Through everything God made, they can clearly see his invisible qualities—his eternal power and divine nature. So they have no excuse for not knowing God.

1:14 1 Cor 9:16
1:16 Acts 3:26 1 Cor 1:18, 24
1:17 †Hab 2:4 Rom 3:21-22 Gal 3:11 Heb 10:38
1:18 Eph 5:6 Col 3:6
1:20 Job 12:7-9 Ps 19:1

1:14 Greek *to Greeks and barbarians.* **1:16** Greek *also the Greek.* **1:17** Or *"The righteous will live by faith."* Hab 2:4. **1:18** Or *who, by their wickedness, prevent the truth from being known.*

• **1:14** What was Paul's obligation? After his experience with Christ on the road to Damascus (Acts 9), his whole life was consumed with spreading the Good News of salvation. His obligation was to people of the entire world. He met his obligation by proclaiming Christ's salvation to people—across all cultural, social, racial, and economic lines, both Jews and Gentiles. We also are obligated to Christ because he took the punishment we deserve for our sins. Although we cannot repay Christ for all he has done, we can demonstrate our gratitude by showing his love to others.

1:15 Paul was eager to preach the gospel. Is our Christian service done in a spirit of eagerness? Or do we serve out of habit, a feeling of obligation, or perhaps even with a feeling of reluctant duty (much like a child who has to take a bath)? When we fully understand what Christ has done for us and what he offers to others, we will be motivated to share the Good News. Ask God to rekindle that fresh eager attitude that wants to obey him and to tell others about Christ.

1:16 Paul was not ashamed because his message was the Good News about Christ. It was a message of salvation, it had life-changing power, and it was for everyone. When you are tempted to be ashamed, remember what the Good News is all about. If you focus on God and on what God is doing in the world rather than on your own inadequacy, you won't be ashamed or embarrassed.

1:16 Why did the message go to the Jews first? They had been God's special people for more than 2,000 years, ever since God chose Abraham and promised great blessings to his descendants (Genesis 12:1-3). God did not choose the Jews because they deserved to be chosen (Deuteronomy 7:7, 8; 9:4-6) but because he wanted to show his love and mercy to them, for it would be through them that his Messiah would come into the world. God chose them, not to play favorites, but so that they would tell the world about his plan of salvation.

For centuries the Jews had been learning about God by obeying his laws, keeping his festivals, and living according to his moral principles. Often they would forget God's promises and laws; often they would have to be disciplined; but still they had a precious heritage of belief in the one true God. Of all the people on earth, the Jews should have been the most ready to welcome the Messiah and to understand his mission and message—and some of them did (see Luke 2:25, 36-38). Of course, the disciples and the great apostle Paul were faithful Jews who recognized in Jesus God's most precious gift to the human race.

1:17 The Good News shows us both how righteous God is in his plan for us to be saved and also how we may be made fit for eternal life. By trusting Christ, our relationship with God is made right. "From start to finish," God declares us to be right with him because of faith and faith alone. Paul then quotes from Habakkuk 2:4 to show that as we trust God, we are saved; we have life both now and forever.

• **1:18** Why is God angry at sinful people? Because they have

substituted the truth about him with a lie (1:25). They have stifled the truth God naturally reveals to all people in order to believe anything that supports their own self-centered lifestyles. God cannot tolerate sin because his nature is morally perfect. He cannot ignore or condone willful rebellion. God wants to remove the sin and restore the sinner—and he is able to, as long as the sinner does not stubbornly distort or reject the truth. But God shows his anger against those who persist in sinning. Make sure you are not pursuing a lie rather than the true God. Don't suppress the truth about him merely to protect your own lifestyle.

1:18ff Romans 1:18–3:20 develops Paul's argument that no one can claim by his or her own efforts or merit to be good in God's sight—not the masses, not the Romans, not even the Jews. All people everywhere deserve God's condemnation for their sin.

1:18-20 In these verses, Paul answers a common objection to belief in God: How could a loving God send anyone to hell, especially someone who has never heard about Christ? In fact, says Paul, God has revealed himself plainly in the creation to *all* people. And yet people reject even this basic knowledge of God. Also, all people have an inner sense of what God requires, but they choose not to live up to it. Put another way, people's moral standards are always better than their behavior. If people suppress God's truth in order to live their own way, they have no excuse. They know the truth, and they will have to endure the consequences of ignoring it.

1:18-20 Some people wonder why we need missionaries if people can know about God through nature (the creation). The answer: (1) Although people know that God exists, their wickedness blinds them to the truth. Missionaries sensitively expose their sin and point them to Christ. (2) Although people may believe there is a God, they refuse to commit themselves to him. Missionaries help persuade them by sharing God's Word and by pointing out the dangerous consequences of their actions. (3) Missionaries help the church obey the great commission of our Lord (Matthew 28:19, 20). (4) Most important, although nature reveals God, people need to be told about Jesus and how, through him, they can have a personal relationship with God.

Knowing that God exists is not enough. People must learn that God is loving and that he sent his Son to demonstrate his love for us (5:8). They must be shown how to accept God's forgiveness of their sins. (See also 10:14, 15.)

1:19 Does anyone have an excuse for not believing in God? The Bible answers an emphatic *no*. God has revealed what he is like in and through his creation. Every person, therefore, either accepts or rejects God. Don't be fooled. When the day comes for God to judge your response to him, no excuses will be accepted. Begin today to give your devotion and worship to him.

1:20 What kind of God does nature reveal? Nature shows us a God of might, intelligence, and intricate detail; a God of order and beauty; a God who controls powerful forces. That is *general* revelation. Through *special* revelation (the Bible and the coming of

1:21
2 Kgs 17:15
Eph 4:17-18

1:22
Jer 10:14
1 Cor 1:20

1:23
Deut 4:15-19
Ps 106:20

1:24
Acts 14:16

1:26
1 Thes 4:5

21 Yes, they knew God, but they wouldn't worship him as God or even give him thanks. And they began to think up foolish ideas of what God was like. As a result, their minds became dark and confused. 22Claiming to be wise, they instead became utter fools. 23And instead of worshiping the glorious, ever-living God, they worshiped idols made to look like mere people and birds and animals and reptiles.

24So God abandoned them to do whatever shameful things their hearts desired. As a result, they did vile and degrading things with each other's bodies. 25 They traded the truth about God for a lie. So they worshiped and served the things God created instead of the Creator himself, who is worthy of eternal praise! Amen. 26That is why God abandoned

---

**WHAT IS
FAITH?**

Faith is a word with many meanings. It can mean faithfulness (Matthew 24:45). It can mean absolute trust, as shown by some of the people who came to Jesus for healing (Luke 7:2-10). It can mean confident hope (Hebrews 11:1). Or, as James points out, it can even mean a barren belief that does not result in good deeds (James 2:14-26). What does Paul mean when, in Romans, he speaks of "saving faith"?

We must be very careful to understand faith as Paul uses the word because he ties faith so closely to salvation. It is *not* something we must do in order to earn salvation—if that were true, then faith would be just one more deed, and Paul clearly states that human deeds can never save us (Galatians 2:16). Instead, faith is a gift God gives us *because* he is saving us (Ephesians 2:8). It is God's grace, not our faith, that saves us. In his mercy, however, when he saves us, he gives us faith—a relationship with his Son that helps us become like him. Through the faith he gives us, he carries us from death into life (John 5:24).

Even in Old Testament times, grace, not deeds, was the basis of salvation. As Hebrews points out, "it is not possible for the blood of bulls and goats to take away sins" (10:4). God intended for his people to look beyond the animal sacrifices to him, but all too often they instead put their confidence in fulfilling the requirements of the law—that is, performing the required sacrifices. When Jesus triumphed over death, he canceled the charges against us and opened the way to the Father (Colossians 2:12-15). Because he is merciful, he offers us faith. How tragic if we turn faith into a deed and try to develop it on our own! We can never come to God through our own faith any more than his Old Testament people could come through their own sacrifices. Instead, we must accept his gracious offer with thanksgiving and allow him to plant the seed of faith within us.

Jesus), we learn about God's love and forgiveness and the promise of eternal life. God has graciously given us many sources that we might come to believe in him.

1:20 God reveals his divine nature and personal qualities through creation, even though creation's testimony has been distorted by the Fall. Adam's sin resulted in a divine curse upon the whole natural order (Genesis 3:17-19); thorns and thistles were an immediate result, and natural disasters have been common from Adam's day to ours. In Romans 8:19-21, Paul says that nature itself is eagerly awaiting its own redemption from the effects of sin (see Revelation 22:3).

1:21-23 How could intelligent people turn to idolatry? Idolatry begins when people reject what they know about God. Instead of looking to him as the creator and sustainer of life, they see themselves as the center of the universe. They soon invent "gods" that are convenient projections of their own selfish ideas. These gods may be wooden figures, or they may also be goals or things we pursue, such as money, power, or possessions. They may even be misrepresentations of God himself—making God in our image, instead of the reverse. The common denominator is this: Idolaters worship the things God made rather than God himself. Is there anything you feel you can't live without? Is there any priority greater than God? Do you have a dream you would sacrifice everything to realize? Does God take first place in your life? Do you worship God or idols of your own making?

• **1:21-32** Paul clearly portrays the inevitable downward spiral into sin. First, people reject God; next, they make up their own ideas of what a god should be and do; then they fall into every kind of wickedness: greed, hate, envy, murder, quarreling, deception, malicious behavior, and gossip. Finally, they grow to hate God and encourage others to do so. God does not cause this steady progression toward evil. Rather, when people reject him, he allows them to live as they choose. God gives them over to or

permits them to experience the natural consequences of their sin. Once caught in the downward spiral, no one can pull himself or herself out. Sinners must trust Christ alone to deliver them from destruction.

1:23 When Paul says that people worshiped idols made to look like people or animals instead of worshiping God, he seems to deliberately state people's wickedness in the terms used in the Genesis narrative of Adam's fall (see Genesis 3:1-24). When people worship the creature instead of the Creator, they lose sight of their own identity as those who are higher than the animals—made in the image of God.

• **1:24-32** These people chose to reject God, and God allowed them to do it. God does not usually stop us from making wrong choices. He lets us choose independence from him, even though he knows that in time we will become slaves to our own rebellious lifestyle and lose our freedom not to sin. Does life without God look like freedom to you? Look more closely. There is no worse slavery than slavery to sin.

• **1:25** People tend to believe lies that reinforce their own selfish, personal beliefs. Today, more than ever, we need to know what the basis is for our beliefs. With TV, music, movies, and the rest of the media often presenting sinful lifestyles and unwholesome values, we find ourselves constantly bombarded by attitudes and beliefs that are totally opposed to the Bible. Be careful about what influences you use to form your opinions. The Bible is the only standard of truth. Evaluate all other opinions in light of its teachings.

1:26, 27 God's plan for sexual relationships is his ideal for his creation. Unfortunately, sin distorts the natural use of God's gifts. Sin often means not only denying God but also denying the way we are made. When people say that any sex act is acceptable as long as nobody gets hurt, they are fooling themselves. In the long run (and often in the short run), sexual sin

them to their shameful desires. Even the women turned against the natural way to have sex and instead indulged in sex with each other. 27And the men, instead of having normal sexual relations with women, burned with lust for each other. Men did shameful things with other men, and as a result of this sin, they suffered within themselves the penalty they deserved.

1:27
Lev 18:22; 20:13
1 Cor 6:9

28Since they thought it foolish to acknowledge God, he abandoned them to their foolish thinking and let them do things that should never be done. 29Their lives became full of every kind of wickedness, sin, greed, hate, envy, murder, quarreling, deception, malicious behavior, and gossip. 30They are backstabbers, haters of God, insolent, proud, and boastful. They invent new ways of sinning, and they disobey their parents. 31They refuse to understand, break their promises, are heartless, and have no mercy. 32They know God's justice requires that those who do these things deserve to die, yet they do them anyway. Worse yet, they encourage others to do them, too.

1:30
2 Tim 3:2
1:31
2 Tim 3:3
1:32
Rom 6:23

God's Judgment of Sin

2 You may think you can condemn such people, but you are just as bad, and you have no excuse! When you say they are wicked and should be punished, you are condemning yourself, for you who judge others do these very same things. 2And we know that God, in his justice, will punish anyone who does such things. 3Since you judge others for doing these things, why do you think you can avoid God's judgment when you do the same things? 4Don't you see how wonderfully kind, tolerant, and patient God is with you? Does this mean nothing to you? Can't you see that his kindness is intended to turn you from your sin?

2:1
Matt 7:1
2:4
Rom 9:22
2 Pet 3:9, 15
2:5
Ps 110:5
2:6
†Ps 62:12
Matt 16:27
2:7
Matt 25:46
2 Tim 4:14

5But because you are stubborn and refuse to turn from your sin, you are storing up terrible punishment for yourself. For a day of anger is coming, when God's righteous judgment will be revealed. 6He will judge everyone according to what they have done. 7He will give

---

hurts people—individuals, families, whole societies. Because sex is such a powerful and essential part of what it means to be human, it must be treated with great respect. Sexual desires are of such importance that the Bible gives them special attention and counsels more careful restraint and self-control than with any other desire. One of the clearest indicators of a society or person in rebellion against God is the rejection of God's guidelines for the use of sex.

1:26, 27 Homosexuality (to turn against or abandon natural relations of sex) was as widespread in Paul's day as it is in ours. God is willing to receive anyone who comes to him in faith, and Christians should love and accept others no matter what their background. Yet, homosexuality is strictly forbidden in Scripture (Leviticus 18:22). Homosexuality is considered an acceptable practice by many in our world today—even by some churches. But society does not set the standard for God's law. Homosexuals believe that their desires are normal and that they have a right to express them. But God does not encourage us to fulfill all our desires (even normal ones). Those desires that violate his laws must be controlled.

If you have these desires, you can and must resist acting upon them. Consciously avoid places or activities you know will kindle temptations. Don't underestimate the power of Satan to tempt you, or the potential for serious harm if you continue to yield to these temptations. Remember, God can and will forgive sexual sins just as he forgives other sins. Surrender yourself to God, asking him to show you the way out of sin and into the light of his freedom and his love. Prayer, Bible study, and loving support of Christians in a Bible-believing church can help you to gain strength to resist these powerful temptations. If you are already deeply involved in homosexual behavior, seek help from a trustworthy, professional, Christian counselor.

• **1:32** How were these people aware that God's justice would require death? All human beings are created in God's image; thus, we have a basic moral nature and a conscience. This truth is understood beyond religious circles. Psychologists, for example, say that the rare person who has no conscience has a serious personality disorder that is extremely difficult to treat. Most people instinctively know when they do wrong—but they may not care. Some people will even risk an early death for the

freedom to indulge their desires now. "I know it's wrong, but I really want it," they say; or "I know it's dangerous, but it's worth the risk." For such people, part of the "fun" is going against God's law, the community's moral standards, common sense, or their own sense of right and wrong. But deep down inside they know that sin deserves the punishment of death (6:23).

2:1 Whenever we find ourselves feeling justifiably angry about someone's sin, we should be careful. We need to speak out against sin, but we must do so in a spirit of humility. Often the sins we notice most clearly in others are the ones that have taken root in us. If we look closely at ourselves, we may find that we are committing the same sins in more socially acceptable forms. For example, a person who gossips may be very critical of others who gossip about him or her.

• **2:1ff** When Paul's letter was read in the Roman church, no doubt many heads nodded as he condemned idol worshipers, homosexual practices, and violent people. But what surprise his listeners must have felt when he turned on them and said in effect, "You are just as bad, and you have no excuse!" Paul was emphatically stressing that we have all sinned repeatedly, and there is no way apart from Christ to be saved from sin's consequences.

• **2:4** In his kindness, God holds back his judgment, giving people time to turn from their sin. It is easy to mistake God's patience for approval of the wrong way we are living. Self-evaluation is difficult, and it is even more difficult to bring ourselves to God and let him tell us where we need to change. But as Christians we must ask God to point out our sins, so that he can heal them. Unfortunately, we are more likely to be amazed at God's patience with others than humbled at his patience with us.

• **2:5-11** Although God does not usually punish us immediately for sin, his eventual judgment is certain. We don't know exactly when it will happen, but we know that no one will escape that final encounter with the Creator. For more on judgment, see John 12:48 and Revelation 20:11-15.

2:7 Paul says that those who patiently and persistently *do* God's will find eternal life. He is not contradicting his previous statement that salvation comes by faith alone (1:16, 17). We are not saved by good deeds, but when we commit our life fully to God,

eternal life to those who keep on doing good, seeking after the glory and honor and immortality that God offers. [8]But he will pour out his anger and wrath on those who live for themselves, who refuse to obey the truth and instead live lives of wickedness. [9]There will be trouble and calamity for everyone who keeps on doing what is evil—for the Jew first and also for the Gentile.* [10]But there will be glory and honor and peace from God for all who do good—for the Jew first and also for the Gentile. [11]For God does not show favoritism.

[12]When the Gentiles sin, they will be destroyed, even though they never had God's written law. And the Jews, who do have God's law, will be judged by that law when they fail to obey it. [13]For merely listening to the law doesn't make us right with God. It is obeying the law that makes us right in his sight. [14]Even Gentiles, who do not have God's written law, show that they know his law when they instinctively obey it, even without having heard it. [15]They demonstrate that God's law is written in their hearts, for their own conscience and thoughts either accuse them or tell them they are doing right. [16]And this is the message I proclaim— that the day is coming when God, through Christ Jesus, will judge everyone's secret life.

The Jews and the Law

[17]You who call yourselves Jews are relying on God's law, and you boast about your special relationship with him. [18]You know what he wants; you know what is right because you have been taught his law. [19]You are convinced that you are a guide for the blind and a light for people who are lost in darkness. [20]You think you can instruct the ignorant and teach children the ways of God. For you are certain that God's law gives you complete knowledge and truth.

[21]Well then, if you teach others, why don't you teach yourself? You tell others not to steal, but do you steal? [22]You say it is wrong to commit adultery, but do you commit adultery? You condemn idolatry, but do you use items stolen from pagan temples?* [23]You are so proud of knowing the law, but you dishonor God by breaking it. [24]No wonder the Scriptures say, "The Gentiles blaspheme the name of God because of you."*

2:9 Greek *also for the Greek;* also in 2:10.   **2:22** Greek *do you steal from temples?*   **2:24** Isa 52:5 (Greek version).

2:8
2 Thes 2:12

2:11
Gal 2:6
Eph 6:9
Col 3:25

2:13
Matt 7:21
John 13:17
Jas 1:22-25

2:14
Acts 10:35

2:16
Acts 10:42
Rom 16:25
2 Tim 2:8

2:17
Mic 3:11

2:20
2 Tim 3:5

2:21
Matt 23:3-4

2:24
†Isa 52:5
Ezek 36:20

SALVATION'S FREEWAY
Verses in Romans that describe the way to salvation.

Romans 3:23 . . . . Everyone has sinned.

Romans 6:23 . . . . The penalty for our sin is death.

Romans 5:8 . . . . Jesus Christ died for sin.

Romans 10:8-10. . . . . To be forgiven for our sin, we must believe and confess that Jesus is Lord. Salvation comes through Jesus Christ.

---

we want to please him and do his will. As such, our good deeds are a grateful *response* to what God has done, not a prerequisite to earning his favor.

• **2:12-15** People are condemned not for what they don't know but for what they do with what they know. Those who know God's written Word and his law will be judged by them. Those who have never seen a Bible still know right from wrong, and they will be judged because they violated those standards that their own consciences dictated. God's law is written within them.

• **2:12-15** If you traveled around the world, you would find evidence in every society and culture of God's moral law. For example, all cultures prohibit murder, and yet in all societies that law has been broken. We belong to a stubborn, sinful race. We know what is right, but we insist on doing what is wrong. It is not enough to know what is right; we must also do it. Admit to yourself and to God that you frequently fail to live up to your own standards (much less to God's standards). That's the first step to forgiveness and healing.

• **2:17ff** Paul continues to argue that all stand guilty before God. After describing the fate of the unbelieving, pagan Gentiles, he moves to admonish God's people. Despite their knowledge of God's will, they were guilty because they, too, refuse to live by it. Those of us who have grown up in Christian families may know what God's Word says. But Paul says that if we do not live up to what we know, we are no better off than unbelievers.

• **2:21, 22** Paul explained to the Jews that they needed to teach *themselves,* not others, by their law. They knew the law so well that they had learned how to excuse their own actions while criticizing others. But the law is more than a set of rules—it is a guideline for living according to God's will. It is also a reminder that we cannot please God without a proper relationship to him. As Jesus pointed out, withholding what rightfully belongs to someone else is stealing (Mark 7:9-13), and anyone who even looks at a woman with lust in his eye has committed adultery with her in his heart (Matthew 5:27, 28). Before we accuse others, we must look at ourselves and see if sin, in any form, exists within us.

• **2:21-27** These verses are a scathing criticism of hypocrisy. It is much easier to tell others how to behave than to behave properly ourselves. It is easier to say the right words than to allow them to take root in our own life. Do you ever advise others to do something you are unwilling to do yourself? Make sure that your actions match your words.

• **2:24** If you claim to be one of God's people, your life should reflect what God is like. When you disobey God, you dishonor his name. People may even blaspheme or profane God's name because of you. What do people think about God as they watch your life?

25 The Jewish ceremony of circumcision has value only if you obey God's law. But if you don't obey God's law, you are no better off than an uncircumcised Gentile. 26 And if the Gentiles obey God's law, won't God declare them to be his own people? 27 In fact, uncircumcised Gentiles who keep God's law will condemn you Jews who are circumcised and possess God's law but don't obey it.

28 For you are not a true Jew just because you were born of Jewish parents or because you have gone through the ceremony of circumcision. 29 No, a true Jew is one whose heart is right with God. And true circumcision is not merely obeying the letter of the law; rather, it is a change of heart produced by God's Spirit. And a person with a changed heart seeks praise* from God, not from people.

2:25
Gal 5:3
2:28
Matt 3:9
John 8:39
Gal 6:15
2:29
Deut 30:6
John 5:44
Rom 7:6
2 Cor 3:6; 10:18
Phil 3:3
Col 2:11
1 Pet 3:4

God Remains Faithful

3 Then what's the advantage of being a Jew? Is there any value in the ceremony of circumcision? 2 Yes, there are great benefits! First of all, the Jews were entrusted with the whole revelation of God.*

3 True, some of them were unfaithful; but just because they were unfaithful, does that mean God will be unfaithful? 4 Of course not! Even if everyone else is a liar, God is true. As the Scriptures say about him,

"You will be proved right in what you say,
and you will win your case in court."*

3:2
Deut 4:7-8
Ps 147:19-20
Acts 7:38
3:4
†Ps 51:4

5 "But," some might say, "our sinfulness serves a good purpose, for it helps people see how righteous God is. Isn't it unfair, then, for him to punish us?" (This is merely a human point of view.) 6 Of course not! If God were not entirely fair, how would he be qualified to judge the world? 7 "But," someone might still argue, "how can God condemn me as a sinner if my dishonesty highlights his truthfulness and brings him more glory?" 8 And some people even slander us by claiming that we say, "The more we sin, the better it is!" Those who say such things deserve to be condemned.

3:5
Rom 5:8
3:7
Rom 9:19
3:8
Rom 6:1

All People Are Sinners

9 Well then, should we conclude that we Jews are better than others? No, not at all, for we have already shown that all people, whether Jews or Gentiles,* are under the power of sin. 10 As the Scriptures say,

3:9
Rom 1:18–2:24
3:10-12
†Pss 14:1-3; 53:1-3

2:29 Or receives praise.   **3:2** Greek the oracles of God.   **3:4** Ps 51:4 (Greek version).   **3:9** Greek or Greeks.

2:25-29 Circumcision refers to the sign of God's special covenant with his people. All Jewish males were required to submit to this rite (Genesis 17:9-14). According to Paul, being a circumcised Jew meant nothing if the person didn't obey God's laws. On the other hand, the uncircumcised Gentiles would receive God's love and approval if they kept God's law. Paul goes on to explain that a true Jew (one who pleases God) is not someone who has been circumcised but someone whose heart is right with God and obeys him.

2:28, 29 To be a Jew meant you were in God's family, an heir to all his promises. Yet Paul made it clear that membership in God's family is based on internal, not external, qualities. All whose hearts are right with God are true Jews—that is, part of God's family (see also Galatians 3:7). Attending church or being baptized, confirmed, or accepted for membership is not enough, just as submitting to circumcision was not enough for the Jews. God desires our heartfelt devotion and obedience (see also Deuteronomy 10:16; Jeremiah 4:4).

• **3:1ff** In this chapter Paul contends that everyone stands guilty before God. Paul has dismantled the common excuses of people who refuse to admit they are sinners: (1) "There is no God" or "I follow my conscience" (1:18-32); (2) "I'm not as bad as other people" (2:1-16); (3) "I'm a church member" or "I'm a religious person" (2:17-29). No one will be exempt from God's judgment of sin. Every person must accept the fact that he or she is sinful and condemned before God and receive God's wonderful gift of salvation.

• **3:1ff** What a depressing picture Paul is painting! All of us—pagan Gentiles, humanitarians, and religious people—are condemned by our own actions. The law, which God gave to show the way to live, holds up our evil deeds to public view. Is there any hope for us? Yes, says Paul. The law condemns us, it is true, but the law is not the basis of our hope. God himself is. He, in his righteousness and wonderful love, offers us eternal life. We receive our salvation not through law but through faith in Jesus Christ. We do not—cannot—earn it; we accept it as a gift from our loving heavenly Father.

3:2 The Jewish nation had great benefits. (1) They were entrusted with God's laws ("the whole revelation of God," Exodus 19–20; Deuteronomy 4:8). (2) They were the race through whom the Messiah came to earth (Isaiah 11:1-10; Matthew 1:1-17). (3) They were the beneficiaries of covenants with God himself (Genesis 17:1-16; Exodus 19:3-6). But these privileges did not make them better than anyone else (see 3:9). In fact, because of them the Jews were even more responsible to live up to God's requirements.

• **3:5-8** Some may think they don't have to worry about sin because (1) it's God's job to forgive; (2) God is so loving that he won't judge; (3) sin isn't so bad—it teaches valuable lessons; or (4) we need to stay in touch with the culture around us. It is far too easy to take God's grace for granted. But God cannot overlook sin. No matter how many excuses they make, sinners will have to answer to God for their sin.

3:10-12 Paul is referring to Psalm 14:1-3. "No one is righteous" means "no one is innocent." Every person is valuable in God's eyes because God created us in his image, and he loves us. But no one is good enough (that is, no one can earn right standing with God). Though we are valuable, we have fallen into sin. But

"No one is righteous—
    not even one.
11 No one is truly wise;
    no one is seeking God.
12 All have turned away;
    all have become useless.
No one does good,
    not a single one."*

3:13
†Pss 5:9; 140:3

13 "Their talk is foul, like the stench from an open grave.
    Their tongues are filled with lies."
"Snake venom drips from their lips."*

3:14
†Ps 10:7

14   "Their mouths are full of cursing and bitterness."*

3:15-17
†Isa 59:7-8

15 "They rush to commit murder.
16   Destruction and misery always follow them.

3:18
†Ps 36:1

17 They don't know where to find peace."*
18   "They have no fear of God at all."*

3:19
Rom 2:12

3:20
Ps 143:2
Rom 4:15; 7:7
Gal 2:16; 3:11

19Obviously, the law applies to those to whom it was given, for its purpose is to keep people from having excuses, and to show that the entire world is guilty before God. 20For no one can ever be made right with God by doing what the law commands. The law simply shows us how sinful we are.

2. Forgiveness of sin through Christ
Christ Took Our Punishment

3:21
Rom 1:2, 17; 9:30

3:22
Rom 4:11; 10:4, 12
Gal 2:16
Col 3:11

21But now God has shown us a way to be made right with him without keeping the requirements of the law, as was promised in the writings of Moses* and the prophets long ago. 22We are made right with God by placing our faith in Jesus Christ. And this is true for everyone who believes, no matter who we are.

3:10-12 Pss 14:1-3; 53:1-3 (Greek version).   **3:13** Pss 5:9 (Greek version); 140:3.   **3:14** Ps 10:7 (Greek version).
3:15-17 Isa 59:7-8.   **3:18** Ps 36:1.   **3:21** Greek *in the law.*

CRUCIAL CONCEPTS IN ROMANS		
ELECTION . . . . Romans 9:10-13	God's choice of an individual or group for a specific purpose or destiny.
JUSTIFICATION . . . . Romans 4:25; 5:18	God's act of declaring us "not guilty" for our sins, making us "right" with him.
PROPITIATION . . . . Romans 3:25	The removal of God's punishment for sin through the perfect sacrifice of Jesus Christ.
REDEMPTION . . . . Romans 3:24; 8:23	Jesus Christ has paid the price so we can go free. The price of sin is death; Jesus paid the price.
SANCTIFICATION . . . . Romans 5:2; 15:16	Becoming more and more like Jesus Christ through the work of the Holy Spirit.
GLORIFICATION . . . . Romans 8:18, 19, 30	The ultimate state of the believer after death when he or she becomes like Christ (1 John 3:2).

God, through Jesus his Son, has redeemed us and offers to forgive us if we turn to him in faith.

• **3:10-18** Paul uses these Old Testament references to show that humanity in general, in its present sinful condition, is unacceptable before God. Have you ever thought to yourself, "Well, I'm not too bad. I'm a pretty good person"? Look at these verses and see if any of them apply to you. Have you ever lied? Have you ever hurt someone's feelings by your words or tone of voice? Are you bitter toward anyone? Do you become angry with those who strongly disagree with you? In thought, word, and deed, you, like everyone else in the world, stand guilty before God. We must remember who we are in his sight—alienated sinners. Don't deny that you are a sinner. Instead, allow your desperate need to point you toward Christ.

• **3:19** The last time someone accused you of wrongdoing, what was your reaction? Denial, argument, and defensiveness? The entire world will be silent before God. No excuses or arguments will remain. Have you reached the point with God where you are ready to hang up your defenses and await his decision? If you haven't, stop now and admit your sin to him. If you have, the following verses are truly good news for you!

3:20, 31 In these verses we see two functions of God's law. First, it shows us where we go wrong. Because of the law, we know that we are helpless sinners and that we must come to Jesus Christ for mercy. Second, the moral code revealed in the law can serve to guide our actions by holding up God's moral standards. We do not earn salvation by keeping the law (no one except Christ ever kept or could keep God's law perfectly), but we do please God when our life conforms to his revealed will for us.

• **3:21-29** After all this bad news about our sinfulness and God's condemnation, Paul gives the wonderful news. There is a way to be declared not guilty—by trusting Jesus Christ to take away our sins. Trusting means putting our confidence in Christ to forgive our sins, to make us right with God, and to empower us to live the way he taught us. God's solution is available to all of us regardless of our background or past behavior.

23For everyone has sinned; we all fall short of God's glorious standard. 24Yet God, with un-deserved kindness, declares that we are righteous. He did this through Christ Jesus when he freed us from the penalty for our sins. 25For God presented Jesus as the sacrifice for sin. Peo-ple are made right with God when they believe that Jesus sacrificed his life, shedding his blood. This sacrifice shows that God was being fair when he held back and did not punish those who sinned in times past, 26for he was looking ahead and including them in what he would do in this present time. God did this to demonstrate his righteousness, for he himself is fair and just, and he declares sinners to be right in his sight when they believe in Jesus.

27Can we boast, then, that we have done anything to be accepted by God? No, because our acquittal is not based on obeying the law. It is based on faith. 28So we are made right with God through faith and not by obeying the law.

29After all, is God the God of the Jews only? Isn't he also the God of the Gentiles? Of course he is. 30There is only one God, and he makes people right with himself only by faith, whether they are Jews or Gentiles.* 31Well then, if we emphasize faith, does this mean that we can forget about the law? Of course not! In fact, only when we have faith do we truly fulfill the law.

3:24
Eph 2:8
Heb 9:12

3:25
Lev 16:10
Heb 9:12-14
1 Pet 1:19
1 Jn 4:10

3:27
Rom 2:17; 4:2
1 Cor 1:29-31

3:28
Acts 13:39

3:29
Rom 10:12
Gal 3:28

3:31
Matt 5:17

The Faith of Abraham

4 Abraham was, humanly speaking, the founder of our Jewish nation. What did he discover about being made right with God? 2If his good deeds had made him acceptable to God, he would have had something to boast about. But that was not God's way. 3For the Scriptures tell us, "Abraham believed God, and God counted him as righteous because of his faith."*

4When people work, their wages are not a gift, but something they have earned. 5But people are counted as righteous, not because of their work, but because of their faith in God

4:2
1 Cor 1:31

4:3
†Gen 15:6
Gal 3:6
Jas 2:23

4:4
Rom 11:6
Gal 2:16

3:30 Greek *whether they are circumcised or uncircumcised.*   **4:3** Gen 15:6.

• **3:23** Some sins seem bigger than others because their obvious consequences are much more serious. Murder, for example, seems to us to be worse than hatred, and adultery seems worse than pride. But this does not mean that because we only commit "little" sins we deserve eternal life. All sins make us sinners, and all sins cut us off from our holy God. All sins, therefore, lead to death (because they disqualify us from living with God), regard-less of how great or small they seem. Don't minimize "little" sins or overrate "big" sins. They all separate us from God, but they all can be forgiven.

• **3:24** Paul explains that God declares that we are righteous. When a judge in a court of law declares the defendant not guilty, all the charges are removed from his record. Legally, it is as if the person had never been accused. When God forgives our sins, our record is wiped clean. From his perspective, it is as though we had never sinned. He could do this because Jesus took the penalty that we deserved. Christ purchased our freedom from sin, and the price was his life.

3:25 Christ died in our place, for our sins. God is justifiably angry at sinners. They have rebelled against him and cut them-selves off from his life-giving power. But God declares Christ's death to be the appropriate, designated sacrifice for our sin. Christ then stands in our place, having paid the penalty of death for our sin, and he completely satisfies God's demands. His sacrifice brings pardon, deliverance, and freedom.

3:25, 26 What happened to people who lived before Christ came and died for sin? If God condemned sinners, was he being unfair? If he saved the righteous, was Christ's sacrifice unnecessary? Paul shows that God forgave all human sin at the cross of Jesus. Old Testament believers looked forward in faith to Christ's coming and were saved, even though they did not know Jesus' name or the details of his earthly life. Unlike the Old Testament believers, you know about the God who loved the world so much that he gave his own Son (John 3:16). Have you put your trust in him?

• **3:27, 28** Most religions require specific duties that must be performed to make a person acceptable to a god. Christianity is unique in that no good deed that we do will make us right with God. No amount of human achievement or personal goodness

will close the gap between God's moral perfection and our imperfect daily performance. Good deeds are important, but they will not earn us eternal life. We are saved only by trusting in what God has done for us (see Ephesians 2:8-10).

• **3:28** Why does God save us by faith alone? (1) Faith eliminates the pride of human effort, because faith is not a deed that we do. (2) Faith exalts what God has done, not what we do. (3) Faith admits that we can't keep the law or measure up to God's stan-dards—we need help. (4) Faith is based on our relationship with God, not our performance for God.

3:31 There were some misunderstandings between the Jewish and Gentile Christians in Rome. Worried Jewish Christians were asking Paul, "Does faith wipe out everything Judaism stands for? Does it cancel our Scriptures, put an end to our customs, declare that God is no longer working through us?" (This is essentially the question used to open chapter 3.) "Of course not!" says Paul. When we understand the way of salvation through faith, we understand the Jewish religion better. We know why Abraham was chosen, why the law was given, and why God worked patiently with Israel for centuries. Faith does not wipe out the Old Testament. Rather, it makes God's dealings with the Jewish people understandable. In chapter 4, Paul will expand on this theme (see also 5:20, 21; 8:3, 4; 13:9, 10; Galatians 3:24-29; and 1 Timothy 1:8 for more on this concept).

4:1-3 The Jews were proud to be descendants of Abraham. Paul uses Abraham as a good example of someone who was saved by faith. By emphasizing faith, Paul is not saying that God's law is unimportant (4:13) but that it is impossible to be saved simply by obeying it. For more about Abraham, see his Profile in Genesis 18, p. 33.

• **4:5** When some people learn that they are saved by God through faith, they start to worry. "Do I have enough faith?" they wonder. "Is my faith strong enough to save me?" These people miss the point. It is Jesus Christ who saves us, not *our* feelings or actions, and he is strong enough to save us no matter how weak our faith is. Jesus offers us salvation as a gift because he loves us, not because we have earned it through our powerful faith. What, then, is the role of faith? Faith is believing and trusting in Jesus Christ and reaching out to accept his wonderful gift of salvation.

who forgives sinners. 6David also spoke of this when he described the happiness of those who are declared righteous without working for it:

4:7-8
†Ps 32:1-2
2 Cor 5:19

7 "Oh, what joy for those
        whose disobedience is forgiven,
        whose sins are put out of sight.
8 Yes, what joy for those
        whose record the LORD has cleared of sin."*

4:9
Gen 15:6
Rom 3:30

9Now, is this blessing only for the Jews, or is it also for uncircumcised Gentiles?* Well, we have been saying that Abraham was counted as righteous by God because of his faith. 10But how did this happen? Was he counted as righteous only after he was circumcised, or was it before he was circumcised? Clearly, God accepted Abraham before he was circumcised!

4:11
Gen 17:10-11

11Circumcision was a sign that Abraham already had faith and that God had already accepted him and declared him to be righteous—even before he was circumcised. So Abraham is the spiritual father of those who have faith but have not been circumcised. They are counted as righteous because of their faith. 12And Abraham is also the spiritual father of those who have been circumcised, but only if they have the same kind of faith Abraham had before he was circumcised.

4:13
Gen 18:18;
22:17-18
Gal 3:29

13Clearly, God's promise to give the whole earth to Abraham and his descendants was based not on his obedience to God's law, but on a right relationship with God that comes by faith. 14If God's promise is only for those who obey the law, then faith is not necessary and the promise is pointless. 15For the law always brings punishment on those who try to obey it. (The only way to avoid breaking the law is to have no law to break!)

4:14
Gal 3:18
4:15
Rom 3:20; 7:12
1 Cor 15:55-56
Gal 3:10
4:16
Gal 3:7

16So the promise is received by faith. It is given as a free gift. And we are all certain to receive it, whether or not we live according to the law of Moses, if we have faith like Abraham's. For Abraham is the father of all who believe. 17That is what the Scriptures mean when God told him, "I have made you the father of many nations."* This happened because Abraham believed in the God who brings the dead back to life and who creates new things out of nothing.

4:17
†Gen 17:5
Isa 48:13
John 5:21
1 Cor 1:28
4:18
†Gen 15:5
4:19
Gen 17:17; 18:11
Heb 11:11

18Even when there was no reason for hope, Abraham kept hoping—believing that he would become the father of many nations. For God had said to him, "That's how many descendants you will have!"* 19And Abraham's faith did not weaken, even though, at about 100 years of age, he figured his body was as good as dead—and so was Sarah's womb.

20Abraham never wavered in believing God's promise. In fact, his faith grew stronger,

4:7-8 Ps 32:1-2 (Greek version). **4:9** Greek *is this blessing only for the circumcised, or is it also for the uncircumcised?* **4:17** Gen 17:5. **4:18** Gen 15:5.

• **4:6-8** What can we do to get rid of guilt? King David was guilty of terrible sins—adultery, murder, lying—and yet he experienced the joy of forgiveness. We, too, can have this joy when we (1) quit denying our guilt and recognize that we have sinned, (2) admit our guilt to God and ask for his forgiveness, and (3) let go of our guilt and believe that God has forgiven us. This can be difficult when a sin has taken root in our life over many years, when it is very serious, or when it involves others. We must remember that Jesus is willing and able to forgive every sin. In view of the tremendous price he paid on the cross, it is arrogant to think that there is any sin too great for him to forgive. Even though our faith is weak, our conscience is sensitive, and our memory haunts us, God's Word declares that sins confessed are sins forgiven (1 John 1:9).

• **4:10-12** Circumcision was a sign to others and a personal seal or certification for the Jews that they were God's special people. Circumcision of all Jewish boys set apart the Jewish people from the nations that worshiped other gods; thus, it was a very important ceremony. God gave the blessing and the command for this ceremony to Abraham (Genesis 17:9-14).

Paul's point here is that the ritual of circumcision did not earn Abraham his acceptance by God; he had been blessed long before the circumcision ceremony was introduced. Abraham found favor with God by faith alone, before he was circumcised. Genesis 12:1-3 tells of God's call to Abraham when he was 75 years old; the circumcision ceremony was introduced when

he was 99 (Genesis 17:1-14). Ceremonies and rituals serve as reminders of our faith as well as instruct new or young believers, but we should not think that they give us any special merit before God. They are outward signs and seals that demonstrate inner belief and trust. The focus of our faith should be on Christ and his saving work, not on our own actions.

4:16 Paul explains that Abraham had pleased God through faith alone before he had ever heard about the rituals that would become so important to the Jewish people. We, too, are saved by faith plus nothing. It is not by loving God and doing good that we are saved; neither is it by faith plus love or by faith plus good deeds. We are saved only through faith in Christ, trusting him to forgive all our sins. For more on Abraham, see his Profile in Genesis 18, p. 33.

4:17 The promise (or covenant) God gave Abraham stated that Abraham would be the father of many nations (Genesis 17:2-4) and that the entire world would be blessed through him (Genesis 12:3). This promise was fulfilled in Jesus Christ. Jesus was from Abraham's line, and truly the whole world was blessed through him.

and in this he brought glory to God. ²¹He was fully convinced that God is able to do whatever he promises. ²²And because of Abraham's faith, God counted him as righteous. ²³And when God counted him as righteous, it wasn't just for Abraham's benefit. It was recorded ²⁴for our benefit, too, assuring us that God will also count us as righteous if we believe in him, the one who raised Jesus our Lord from the dead. ²⁵He was handed over to die because of our sins, and he was raised to life to make us right with God.

Faith Brings Joy

5 Therefore, since we have been made right in God's sight by faith, we have peace with God because of what Jesus Christ our Lord has done for us. ²Because of our faith, Christ has brought us into this place of undeserved privilege where we now stand, and we confidently and joyfully look forward to sharing God's glory.

³We can rejoice, too, when we run into problems and trials, for we know that they help us develop endurance. ⁴And endurance develops strength of character, and character strengthens our confident hope of salvation. ⁵And this hope will not lead to disappointment. For we know how dearly God loves us, because he has given us the Holy Spirit to fill our hearts with his love.

⁶When we were utterly helpless, Christ came at just the right time and died for us sinners. ⁷Now, most people would not be willing to die for an upright person, though someone might perhaps be willing to die for a person who is especially good. ⁸But God showed his great love for us by sending Christ to die for us while we were still sinners. ⁹And since we have been made right in God's sight by the blood of Christ, he will certainly save us from God's condemnation. ¹⁰For since our friendship with God was restored by the death of his Son while we were still his enemies, we will certainly be saved through the life of his Son. ¹¹So now we can rejoice in our wonderful new relationship with God because our Lord Jesus Christ has made us friends of God.

4:22
†Gen 15:6
Rom 4:3

4:24
1 Pet 1:21

4:25
Isa 53:4-5
Rom 8:30
1 Cor 15:17
2 Cor 5:15
1 Pet 1:21

5:1
Rom 3:28

5:2
Eph 2:18; 3:12

5:3
Matt 5:12

5:5
2 Cor 1:22
Gal 4:6
Eph 1:13
Phil 1:20

5:6
Gal 4:4
Eph 5:2

5:8
John 3:16
1 Jn 4:10

5:9
Rom 1:18; 2:5, 8

5:10
Rom 8:34
2 Cor 5:18-19
Eph 2:3

• **4:21** Abraham never doubted that God would fulfill his promise. Abraham's life was marked by mistakes, sins, and failures as well as by wisdom and goodness, but he consistently trusted God. His faith was strengthened by the obstacles he faced, and his life was an example of faith in action. If he had looked only at his own resources for subduing Canaan and founding a nation, he would have given up in despair. But Abraham looked to God, obeyed him, and waited for God to fulfill his word.

• **4:25** When we accept Jesus Christ as our Savior, an exchange takes place. We give him our sins, and he forgives us and makes us right with God (see 2 Corinthians 5:21). There is nothing we can do to earn this. Only through Christ can we be made right in God's eyes. What an incredible bargain this is for us! But sadly, many still choose to pass up this gift to continue "enjoying" their sin.

• **5:1** We are now at peace *with God,* which may differ from peaceful feelings such as calmness and tranquility. Peace with God means that we have been reconciled with him. There is no more hostility between us, no sin blocking our relationship with him. Peace with God is possible only because Jesus paid the price for our sins through his death on the cross.

5:1-5 These verses introduce a section that contains some difficult concepts. To understand the next four chapters, it helps to keep in mind the two-sided reality of the Christian life. On the one hand, we are complete in Christ (our acceptance with him is secure). On the other hand, we are growing in Christ (we are becoming more and more like him). At one and the same time we have the status of kings and the duties of slaves. We feel both the presence of Christ and the pressure of sin. We enjoy the peace that comes from being made right with God, but we still face daily problems that often help us grow. If we remember these two sides of the Christian life, we will not grow discouraged as we face temptations and problems. Instead, we will learn to depend on the power available to us from Christ, who lives in us by the Holy Spirit.

5:2 Paul states that, as believers, we now have entered into a place of undeserved privilege. Not only has God declared us not guilty; he has drawn us close to himself. Instead of being enemies, we have become his friends—in fact, his own children (John 15:15; Galatians 4:5).

• **5:3, 4** For first-century Christians, suffering was the rule rather than the exception. Paul tells us that in the future we will *become,* but until then we must *overcome.* This means we will experience difficulties that help us grow. We rejoice in suffering, not because we like pain or deny its tragedy, but because we know God is using life's difficulties and Satan's attacks to build our character. The problems that we run into will develop our perseverance—which in turn will strengthen our character, deepen our trust in God, and give us greater confidence about the future. You probably find your patience tested in some way every day. Thank God for those opportunities to grow, and deal with them in his strength (see also James 1:2-4; 1 Peter 1:6, 7).

5:5, 6 All three members of the Trinity are involved in salvation. The Father loved us so much that he sent his Son to bridge the gap between us (John 3:16). The Father and the Son send the Holy Spirit to fill our life with love and to enable us to live by his power (Acts 1:8). With all this loving care, how can we do less than serve him completely!

• **5:6** We were weak and helpless because we could do nothing on our own to save ourselves. Someone had to come and rescue us. Christ came at exactly the right time in history—according to God's own schedule. God controls all history, and he controlled the timing, method, and events surrounding Jesus' death.

• **5:8** *While we were still sinners*—these are amazing words. God sent Jesus Christ to die for us, not because we were good enough, but just because he loved us. Whenever you feel uncertain about God's love for you, remember that he loved you even before you turned to him.

• **5:9, 10** The love that caused Christ to die is the same love that sends the Holy Spirit to live in us and guide us every day. The power that raised Christ from the dead is the same power that saved you and is available to you in your daily life. Be assured that, having begun a life with Christ, you have a reserve of power and love to call on each day for help to meet every challenge or trial. You can pray for God's power and love as you need it.

• **5:11** God is holy, and he will not be associated with sin. All people are sinful and so they are separated from God. In addition,

Adam and Christ Contrasted

5:12
Gen 2:17; 3:19
1 Cor 15:21-22

5:13
Rom 4:15

5:14
1 Cor 15:22, 45

5:17
1 Cor 15:21

5:18
Isa 53:11
1 Cor 15:22

5:19
Phil 2:8

5:20
Rom 4:15; 7:8
Gal 3:19

5:21
Rom 6:23

¹²When Adam sinned, sin entered the world. Adam's sin brought death, so death spread to everyone, for everyone sinned. ¹³Yes, people sinned even before the law was given. But it was not counted as sin because there was not yet any law to break. ¹⁴Still, everyone died—from the time of Adam to the time of Moses—even those who did not disobey an explicit commandment of God, as Adam did. Now Adam is a symbol, a representation of Christ, who was yet to come. ¹⁵But there is a great difference between Adam's sin and God's gracious gift. For the sin of this one man, Adam, brought death to many. But even greater is God's wonderful grace and his gift of forgiveness to many through this other man, Jesus Christ. ¹⁶And the result of God's gracious gift is very different from the result of that one man's sin. For Adam's sin led to condemnation, but God's free gift leads to our being made right with God, even though we are guilty of many sins. ¹⁷For the sin of this one man, Adam, caused death to rule over many. But even greater is God's wonderful grace and his gift of righteousness, for all who receive it will live in triumph over sin and death through this one man, Jesus Christ.

¹⁸Yes, Adam's one sin brings condemnation for everyone, but Christ's one act of righteousness brings a right relationship with God and new life for everyone. ¹⁹Because one person disobeyed God, many became sinners. But because one other person obeyed God, many will be made righteous.

²⁰God's law was given so that all people could see how sinful they were. But as people sinned more and more, God's wonderful grace became more abundant. ²¹So just as sin ruled over all people and brought them to death, now God's wonderful grace rules instead, giving us right standing with God and resulting in eternal life through Jesus Christ our Lord.

WHAT WE HAVE AS GOD'S CHILDREN

What we have as Adam's children	What we have as God's children
Ruin 5:9	Rescue 5:8
Sin 5:12, 15, 21	Righteousness 5:18
Death 5:12, 16, 21	Eternal life 5:17, 21
Separation from God 5:18	Relationship with God 5:11, 19
Disobedience 5:12, 19	Obedience 5:19
Judgment 5:18	Deliverance 5:10, 11
Law 5:20	Grace 5:20

---

all sin deserves punishment. Instead of punishing us with the death we deserve, however, Christ took our sins upon himself and took our punishment by dying on the cross. Now we can rejoice in God. Through faith in *Christ's* work, we become close to God (friends) rather than being enemies and outcasts.

• **5:12** How can we be declared guilty for something Adam did thousands of years ago? Many feel it isn't fair for God to judge us because of Adam's sin. Yet each of us confirms our heritage with Adam by our own sins every day. We have the same sinful nature and are prone to rebel against God, and we are judged for the sins *we* commit. Because we are sinners, it isn't fairness we need—it is mercy.

• **5:13, 14** Paul has shown that keeping the law does not bring salvation. Here he adds that breaking the law is not what brings death. Death is the result of Adam's sin and of the sins we all commit, even if they don't resemble Adam's. Paul reminds his readers that for thousands of years the law had not yet been explicitly given, and yet people died. The law was added, he explains in 5:20, to help people see their sinfulness, to show them the seriousness of their offenses, and to drive them to God for mercy and pardon. This was true in Moses' day, and it is still true today. Sin is a deep discrepancy between who we are and who we were created to be. The law points out our sin and places the responsibility for it squarely on our shoulders. But the law offers no remedy. When we are convicted of sin, we must turn to Jesus Christ for healing.

• **5:14** Adam was the counterpart of Christ. Just as Adam was a representative of created humanity, so is Christ the representative of a new spiritual humanity.

• **5:15-19** We were all born into Adam's physical family—the family line that leads to certain death. All of us have reaped the results of Adam's sin. We have inherited his guilt, a sinful nature (the tendency to sin), and God's punishment. Because of Jesus, however, we can trade judgment for forgiveness. Christ offers us the opportunity to be born into his spiritual family—the family line that begins with forgiveness and leads to eternal life. If we do nothing, we receive death through Adam; but if we come to God by faith, we receive life through Christ. To which family line do you now belong?

• **5:20** As a sinner, separated from God, you see his law from below, as a ladder to be climbed to get to God. Perhaps you have repeatedly tried to climb it, only to fall to the ground every time you have advanced one or two rungs. Or perhaps the sheer height of the ladder seems so overwhelming that you have never even started up. In either case, what relief you should feel to see Jesus offering with open arms to lift you above the ladder of the law, to take you directly to God! Once Jesus lifts you into God's presence, you are free to obey—out of love, not necessity, and through God's power, not your own. You know that if you stumble, you will not fall back to the ground. Instead, you will be caught and held in Christ's loving arms.

3. Freedom from sin's grasp
Sin's Power Is Broken

6 Well then, should we keep on sinning so that God can show us more and more of his wonderful grace? ²Of course not! Since we have died to sin, how can we continue to live in it? ³Or have you forgotten that when we were joined with Christ Jesus in baptism, we joined him in his death? ⁴For we died and were buried with Christ by baptism. And just as Christ was raised from the dead by the glorious power of the Father, now we also may live new lives.

⁵Since we have been united with him in his death, we will also be raised to life as he was. ⁶We know that our old sinful selves were crucified with Christ so that sin might lose its power in our lives. We are no longer slaves to sin. ⁷For when we died with Christ we were set free from the power of sin. ⁸And since we died with Christ, we know we will also live with him. ⁹We are sure of this because Christ was raised from the dead, and he will never die again. Death no longer has any power over him. ¹⁰When he died, he died once to break the power of sin. But now that he lives, he lives for the glory of God. ¹¹So you also should consider yourselves to be dead to the power of sin and alive to God through Christ Jesus.

¹²Do not let sin control the way you live;* do not give in to sinful desires. ¹³Do not let any part of your body become an instrument of evil to serve sin. Instead, give yourselves completely to God, for you were dead, but now you have new life. So use your whole body as an instrument to do what is right for the glory of God. ¹⁴Sin is no longer your master, for you no longer live under the requirements of the law. Instead, you live under the freedom of God's grace.

6:1
Rom 3:5-8
6:2
Rom 8:13
Col 2:20; 3:3
6:4
Eph 4:22-24
Col 2:12; 3:10
6:5
Phil 3:10-11
Col 2:12; 3:1
6:6
Gal 2:20; 5:24
Col 2:12
6:7
1 Pet 4:1
6:11
Rom 7:4
Col 2:20; 3:3
6:13
Rom 12:1
2 Cor 5:14
6:14
Rom 7:4, 6; 8:2, 12
Gal 5:18
1 Jn 3:16

6:12 Or *Do not let sin reign in your body, which is subject to death.*

6:1–8:39 This section deals with *sanctification*—the change God makes in our life as we grow in the faith. Chapter 6 explains that believers are free from sin's control. Chapter 7 discusses the continuing struggle believers have with sin. Chapter 8 describes how we can have victory over sin.

- **6:1, 2** If God loves to forgive, why not give him more to forgive? If forgiveness is guaranteed, do we have the freedom to sin as much as we want to? Paul's forceful answer is *Of course not!* Such an attitude—deciding ahead of time to take advantage of God—shows that a person does not understand the seriousness of sin. God's forgiveness does not make sin less serious; his Son's death for sin shows us the dreadful seriousness of sin. Jesus paid with his life so we could be forgiven. The availability of God's mercy must not become an excuse for careless living and moral laxness.

- **6:1-4** In the church of Paul's day, immersion was the usual form of baptism; that is, new Christians were completely "buried" in water. They understood baptism to symbolize the death and burial of the old way of life. Coming up out of the water symbolized resurrection to new life with Christ. If we think of our old, sinful life as dead and buried, we have a powerful motive to resist sin. We can consciously choose to treat the desires and temptations of the old nature as if they were dead. Then we can continue to enjoy our wonderful new life with Jesus (see Galatians 3:27 and Colossians 2:12 and 3:1-4 for more on this concept).

6:5ff Because we are united with Christ in his death, our evil desires and bondage to sin died with him. Now, united by faith with him in his resurrection life, we have unbroken fellowship with God and freedom from sin's hold on us. For more on the difference between our new life in Christ and our old sinful nature, read Ephesians 4:21-24 and Colossians 3:3-15.

- **6:6, 7** The power of sin over us died with Christ on the cross. Our "old sinful selves," our sinful nature, died once and for all, so we are freed from its power. The "power of sin" refers to our rebellious sin-loving nature inherited from Adam. Though we often willingly cooperate with our sinful nature, it is not us but the sin in us that is evil. And it is this power of sin at work in our life that is defeated. Paul has already stated that through faith

in Christ we stand righteous before God. Here Paul emphasizes that we need no longer live under sin's power. God does not take us out of the world or make us robots—we will still feel like sinning, and sometimes we will sin. The difference is that before we were saved we were slaves to our sinful nature, but now we can choose to live for Christ (see Galatians 2:20).

- **6:8, 9** Because of Christ's death and resurrection, his followers need never fear death. That assurance frees us to enjoy fellowship with him and to do his will. This will affect all our activities—work and worship, play, Bible study, quiet times, and times of caring for others. When you know that you don't have to fear death, you will experience a new vigor in life.

- **6:11** "Consider yourselves to be dead to the power of sin" means that we should regard our old sinful nature as dead and unresponsive to sin. Because of our union and identification with Christ, we no longer want to pursue our old plans, desires, and goals. Now we want to live for the glory of God. As we start this new life, the Holy Spirit will help us become all that Christ wants us to be.

6:12 How can we keep this command to not let sin control the way we live, to not give in to its desires? We can take the following steps: (1) Identify our personal weaknesses, (2) recognize the things that tempt us, (3) stay away from sources of temptation, (4) practice self-restraint, (5) consciously invest our time in good habits and service, and (5) lean on God's strength and grace.

6:13 When Paul uses the term "instrument of evil," he uses a word that can refer to a tool or a weapon. Our skills, capabilities, and bodies can serve many purposes, good or bad. In sin, every part of our bodies are vulnerable. In Christ, every part can be an instrument for service. It is the one to whom we offer our service that makes the difference. We are like lasers that can burn destructive holes in steel plates or do delicate cataract surgery. Will you give yourself completely to God, asking him to put you to good use for his glory?

- **6:14, 15** If we're no longer under the law but under grace, are we now free to sin and disregard the Ten Commandments? Paul says, "Of course not!" When we were under the law, sin was our master—the law does not justify us or help us overcome sin. But now that we are bound to Christ, he is our Master, and he gives us power to do good rather than evil.

6:16
John 8:34
2 Pet 2:19
6:17
2 Tim 1:13
6:18
John 8:32
6:21
Rom 7:5; 8:6, 13
6:22
John 8:32
Rom 8:2
1 Cor 7:22
1 Pet 1:9; 2:16
6:23
Matt 25:46
John 3:16; 17:2
Rom 5:21
Gal 6:8

¹⁵Well then, since God's grace has set us free from the law, does that mean we can go on sinning? Of course not! ¹⁶Don't you realize that you become the slave of whatever you choose to obey? You can be a slave to sin, which leads to death, or you can choose to obey God, which leads to righteous living. ¹⁷Thank God! Once you were slaves of sin, but now you wholeheartedly obey this teaching we have given you. ¹⁸Now you are free from your slavery to sin, and you have become slaves to righteous living.

¹⁹Because of the weakness of your human nature, I am using the illustration of slavery to help you understand all this. Previously, you let yourselves be slaves to impurity and lawlessness, which led ever deeper into sin. Now you must give yourselves to be slaves to righteous living so that you will become holy.

²⁰When you were slaves to sin, you were free from the obligation to do right. ²¹And what was the result? You are now ashamed of the things you used to do, things that end in eternal doom. ²²But now you are free from the power of sin and have become slaves of God. Now you do those things that lead to holiness and result in eternal life. ²³For the wages of sin is death, but the free gift of God is eternal life through Christ Jesus our Lord.

No Longer Bound to the Law

7:2
1 Cor 7:39

7 Now, dear brothers and sisters*—you who are familiar with the law—don't you know that the law applies only while a person is living? ²For example, when a woman marries,

7:1 Greek *brothers;* also in 7:4.

WHAT HAS GOD DONE ABOUT SIN?	He has given us		Principle	Importance
	New life	6:2, 3	Sin's power is broken.	We can be certain that sin's power is broken.
		6:4	Sin-loving nature is buried.	
		6:6	You are no longer under sin's control.	
	New nature	6:5	Now you share his new life.	We can see ourselves as unresponsive to the old power and alive to the new.
		6:11	Look upon your old self as dead; instead, be alive to God.	
	New freedom	6:12	Do not let sin control you.	We can commit ourselves to obey Christ in perfect freedom.
		6:13	Give yourselves completely to God.	
		6:14	You are free.	
		6:16	You can choose your own master.	

• **6:16-18** All people have a master and pattern themselves after him. Without Jesus, we would have no choice; we would be enslaved to sin, and the results would be guilt, suffering, and separation from God. Thanks to Jesus, however, we can now choose God as our Master. Following him, we can enjoy new life and learn how to work for him. Are you still serving your first master, sin? Or have you chosen God?

• **6:17** To "wholeheartedly obey" means to give yourself fully to God, to love him "with all your heart, all your soul, and all your mind" (Matthew 22:37). And yet so often our efforts to know and obey God's commands can best be described as "halfhearted." How do you rate your heart's obedience? God wants to give you the power to obey him with all your heart.

6:17 The "teaching" they were to obey refers to the Good News that Jesus died for their sins and was raised to give them new life. Many believe that this refers to the early church's statement of faith found in 1 Corinthians 15:1-11.

• **6:19-22** It is impossible to be neutral. Every person has a master—either God or sin. A Christian is not someone who cannot sin but someone who is no longer a slave to sin. He or she belongs to God.

• **6:23** You are free to choose between two masters, but you are not free to adjust the consequences of your choice. Each of the two masters pays with his own kind of currency. The currency of sin is eternal death. That is all you can expect or hope for in life without God. Christ's currency is eternal life—new life with God

that begins on earth and continues forever with God. What choice have you made?

6:23 Eternal life is a gift from God. If it is a gift, then it is not something that we earn, nor something that must be paid back. Consider the foolishness of someone who receives a gift given out of love and then offers to pay for it. A gift cannot be purchased by the recipient. A more appropriate response to a loved one who offers a gift is graceful acceptance with gratitude. Our salvation is a gift of God, not something of our own doing (Ephesians 2:8, 9). He saved us because of his mercy, not because of any good things that we have done (Titus 3:5). How much more we should accept with thanksgiving the gift that God has freely given to us.

• **7:1ff** Paul shows that the law is powerless to save the sinner (7:7-14), the lawkeeper (7:15-22), and even the person with a new nature (7:23-25). The sinner is condemned by the law; the law-keeper can't live up to it; and the person with the new nature finds his or her obedience to the law sabotaged by the effects of the old nature. Once again Paul declares that salvation cannot be found by obeying the law. No matter who we are, only Jesus Christ can set us free.

• **7:2-6** Paul uses marriage to illustrate our relationship to the law. When a spouse dies, the law of marriage no longer applies. Because we have died with Christ, the law can no longer condemn us. Since we are united with Christ, his Spirit enables us to produce good deeds for God. We now serve God, not by obeying a set of rules, but out of renewed hearts and minds that overflow with love for him.

the law binds her to her husband as long as he is alive. But if he dies, the laws of marriage no longer apply to her. ³So while her husband is alive, she would be committing adultery if she married another man. But if her husband dies, she is free from that law and does not commit adultery when she remarries.

⁴So, my dear brothers and sisters, this is the point: You died to the power of the law when you died with Christ. And now you are united with the one who was raised from the dead. As a result, we can produce a harvest of good deeds for God. ⁵When we were controlled by our old nature,* sinful desires were at work within us, and the law aroused these evil desires that produced a harvest of sinful deeds, resulting in death. ⁶But now we have been released from the law, for we died to it and are no longer captive to its power. Now we can serve God, not in the old way of obeying the letter of the law, but in the new way of living in the Spirit.

God's Law Reveals Our Sin

⁷Well then, am I suggesting that the law of God is sinful? Of course not! In fact, it was the law that showed me my sin. I would never have known that coveting is wrong if the law had not said, "You must not covet."* ⁸But sin used this command to arouse all kinds of covetous desires within me! If there were no law, sin would not have that power. ⁹At one time I lived without understanding the law. But when I learned the command not to covet, for instance, the power of sin came to life, ¹⁰and I died. So I discovered that the law's commands, which were supposed to bring life, brought spiritual death instead. ¹¹Sin took advantage of those commands and deceived me; it used the commands to kill me. ¹²But still, the law itself is holy, and its commands are holy and right and good.

¹³But how can that be? Did the law, which is good, cause my death? Of course not! Sin used what was good to bring about my condemnation to death. So we can see how terrible sin really is. It uses God's good commands for its own evil purposes.

Struggling with Sin

¹⁴So the trouble is not with the law, for it is spiritual and good. The trouble is with me, for I am all too human, a slave to sin. ¹⁵I don't really understand myself, for I want to do what is

7:5 Greek *When we were in the flesh.* **7:7** Exod 20:17; Deut 5:21.

7:3
Luke 16:18
7:4
Rom 6:6; 8:2
Gal 5:18
Col 2:14
1 Pet 2:24
7:5
Rom 6:21; 8:8
Gal 5:19-21
7:6
2 Cor 3:6
Gal 5:22
Phil 3:3
7:7
†Exod 20:17
†Deut 5:21
Rom 4:15
7:8
Rom 4:15
7:10
Lev 18:5
Rom 10:5
Gal 3:12
7:11
Gen 3:13
Heb 3:13
7:12
1 Tim 1:8
7:14
1 Kgs 21:20-25
Rom 3:9; 6:6
7:15
Gal 5:17

● **7:4** When a person dies to the old life and accepts Christ as Savior, a new life begins. An unbeliever's life is centered on his or her own personal gratification. Those who don't follow Christ have only their own self-determination as their source of power. By contrast, God is at the center of a Christian's life. God supplies the power for a Christian's daily living. Believers find that their whole way of looking at the world changes when they come to Christ.

● **7:6** Some people try to earn their way to God by keeping a set of rules (obeying the Ten Commandments, attending church faithfully, or doing good deeds), but all they earn for their efforts is frustration and discouragement. However, because of Christ's sacrifice, the way to God is already open, and we can become his children simply by putting our faith in him. No longer trying to reach God by keeping rules, we can become more and more like Jesus as we live for him day by day. Let the Holy Spirit turn your eyes away from your own performance and toward Jesus. He will free you to serve him out of love and gratitude. This is "living in the Spirit."

● **7:6** Keeping the rules, laws, and customs of Christianity doesn't save us. Even if we could keep our actions pure, we would still be doomed because our hearts and minds are perverse and rebellious. Like Paul, we can find no relief in the synagogue or church until we look to Jesus Christ himself for our salvation—which he gives us freely. When we do come to Jesus, we are flooded with relief and gratitude. Will we keep the rules any better? Most likely, but we will be motivated by love and gratitude, not by the desire to get God's approval. We will not be merely submitting to an external code, but we will willingly and lovingly seek to do God's will.

● **7:9-11** Where there is no law, there is no sin, because people cannot know that their actions are sinful unless a law forbids those actions. God's law makes people realize that they are sinners doomed to die, yet it offers no help. Sin is real, and it is dangerous. Imagine a sunny day at the beach. You plunge into the surf; then you notice a sign on the pier: "No swimming. Sharks."

Your day is ruined. Is it the sign's fault? Are you angry with the people who put it up? The law is like the sign. It is essential, and we are grateful for it—but it doesn't get rid of the sharks.

● **7:11, 12** Sin deceives people by misusing the law. The law was holy, expressing God's nature and will for people. In the Garden of Eden (Genesis 3), the serpent deceived Eve, changing her focus from the freedom she had to the one restriction God had made. Ever since then, we have all been rebels. Sin looks good to us precisely because God has said it is wrong. When we are tempted to rebel, we need to look at the law from a wider perspective—in the light of God's grace and mercy. If we focus on his great love for us, we will understand that he only restricts us from actions and attitudes that ultimately will harm us.

● **7:15** Paul shares three lessons that he learned in trying to deal with his sinful desires: (1) Knowledge of the rules is not the answer (7:9). Paul felt fine as long as he did not understand what the law demanded. When he learned the truth, he knew he was doomed. (2) Self-determination (struggling in one's own strength) doesn't succeed (7:15). Paul found himself sinning in ways that weren't even attractive to him. (3) Becoming a Christian does not stamp out all sin and temptation from a person's life (7:22-25).

Being born again takes a moment of faith, but becoming like Christ is a lifelong process. Paul compares Christian growth to a strenuous race or fight (1 Corinthians 9:24-27; 2 Timothy 4:7). Thus, as Paul has been emphasizing since the beginning of this letter, *no one* in the world is innocent; no one deserves to be saved—not the pagan who doesn't know God's laws, not the person who knows them and tries to keep them. All of us must depend totally on the work of Christ for our salvation. We cannot earn it by our good behavior.

● **7:15** This is more than the cry of one desperate man; it describes the experience of all Christians struggling against sin or trying to please God by keeping rules and laws without the Spirit's help. We must never underestimate the power of sin and attempt to fight it in

right, but I don't do it. Instead, I do what I hate. ¹⁶But if I know that what I am doing is wrong, this shows that I agree that the law is good. ¹⁷So I am not the one doing wrong; it is sin living in me that does it.

¹⁸And I know that nothing good lives in me, that is, in my sinful nature.* I want to do what is right, but I can't. ¹⁹I want to do what is good, but I don't. I don't want to do what is wrong, but I do it anyway. ²⁰But if I do what I don't want to do, I am not really the one doing wrong; it is sin living in me that does it.

²¹I have discovered this principle of life—that when I want to do what is right, I inevitably do what is wrong. ²²I love God's law with all my heart. ²³But there is another power* within me that is at war with my mind. This power makes me a slave to the sin that is still within me. ²⁴Oh, what a miserable person I am! Who will free me from this life that is dominated by sin and death? ²⁵Thank God! The answer is in Jesus Christ our Lord. So you see how it is: In my mind I really want to obey God's law, but because of my sinful nature I am a slave to sin.

Life in the Spirit

8 So now there is no condemnation for those who belong to Christ Jesus. ²And because you belong to him, the power* of the life-giving Spirit has freed you* from the power of sin that leads to death. ³The law of Moses was unable to save us because of the weakness of our sinful nature.* So God did what the law could not do. He sent his own Son in a body like the bodies we sinners have. And in that body God declared an end to sin's control over us by giving his Son as a sacrifice for our sins. ⁴He did this so that the just requirement of the law would be fully satisfied for us, who no longer follow our sinful nature but instead follow the Spirit.

⁵Those who are dominated by the sinful nature think about sinful things, but those who are controlled by the Holy Spirit think about things that please the Spirit. ⁶So letting your sinful nature control your mind leads to death. But letting the Spirit control your mind leads to life and peace. ⁷For the sinful nature is always hostile to God. It never did obey God's laws, and it never will. ⁸That's why those who are still under the control of their sinful nature can never please God.

⁹But you are not controlled by your sinful nature. You are controlled by the Spirit if you have the Spirit of God living in you. (And remember that those who do not have the Spirit of

7:18
Gen 6:5; 8:21
John 3:6
Rom 8:3

7:22
Pss 1:2; 40:8

7:23
Gal 5:17
Jas 4:1
1 Pet 2:11

7:24
Rom 6:6; 8:2

7:25
Rom 6:16, 22
1 Cor 15:57
2 Cor 2:14

8:1
Rom 8:34

8:2
Rom 8:11
2 Cor 3:6
Gal 2:19; 5:1

8:3
Acts 13:38
2 Cor 5:21
Phil 2:7
Heb 2:14; 4:15

8:4
Gal 5:16, 25

8:5
Gal 5:19-22

8:6
Rom 6:23
Gal 6:8

8:9
John 14:17-18, 23
Gal 4:6
Phil 1:19
1 Pet 1:11

7:18 Greek *my flesh;* also in 7:25. **7:23** Greek *law;* also in 7:23b. **8:2a** Greek *the law;* also in 8:2b. **8:2b** Some manuscripts read *me.* **8:3** Greek *our flesh;* similarly in 8:4, 5, 6, 7, 8, 9, 12.

---

our own strength. Satan is a crafty tempter, and we have an amazing ability to make excuses. Instead of trying to overcome sin with our own human willpower, we must take hold of God's provision for victory over sin: the Holy Spirit, who lives within us and gives us power. And when we fall, he lovingly reaches out to help us up.

7:23-25 The "power within" is the sin nature deep within us. This is our vulnerability to sin; it refers to everything within us that is more loyal to our old way of selfish living than to God.

• **7:23-25** There is great tension in daily Christian experience. The conflict is that we agree with God's commands but cannot do them. As a result, we are painfully aware of our sin. This inward struggle with sin was as real for Paul as it is for us. From Paul we learn what to do about it. Whenever he felt overwhelmed by the spiritual battle, he would return to the beginnings of his spiritual life, remembering how he had been freed from sin by Jesus Christ. When we feel confused and overwhelmed by sin's appeal, let us claim the freedom Christ gave us. His power can lift us to victory.

• **8:1** "Not guilty; let him go free." What would those words mean to you if you were on death row? The fact is that the whole human race *is* on death row, justly condemned for repeatedly breaking God's holy law. Without Jesus we would have no hope at all. But thank God! He has declared us not guilty and has offered us freedom from sin and power to do his will.

8:2 This life-giving Spirit is the Holy Spirit. He was present at the creation of the world (Genesis 1:2), and he is the power behind the rebirth of every Christian. He gives us the power we need to live the Christian life. For more about the Holy Spirit, read the notes on John 3:6; Acts 1:3; 1:4, 5; 1:5.

8:3 Jesus gave himself as a sacrifice for our sins. In Old Testa-

ment times, animal sacrifices were continually offered at the Temple. The sacrifices showed the Israelites the seriousness of sin: Blood had to be shed before sins could be pardoned (see Leviticus 17:11). But the blood of animals could not really remove sins (Hebrews 10:4). The sacrifices could only point to Jesus' sacrifice, which paid the penalty for all sins.

• **8:5, 6** Paul divides people into two categories: those who are dominated by their sinful nature, and those who are controlled by the Holy Spirit. All of us would be in the first category if Jesus hadn't offered us a way out. Once we have said yes to Jesus, we will want to continue following him, because his way brings life and peace. Daily we must consciously choose to center our life on God. Use the Bible to discover God's guidelines, and then follow them. In every perplexing situation, ask yourself, What would Jesus want me to do? When the Holy Spirit points out what is right, do it eagerly. For more on our sinful nature versus our new life in Christ, see 6:6-8; Ephesians 4:22-24; Colossians 3:3-15.

• **8:9** Have you ever worried about whether or not you really are a Christian? A Christian is anyone who has the Spirit of God living in him or her. If you have sincerely trusted Christ for your salvation and acknowledged him as Lord, then the Holy Spirit lives within you and you are a Christian. You can be assured that you have the Holy Spirit because Jesus promised that he would send him. Since you now believe that Jesus Christ is God's Son and that eternal life comes through him (1 John 5:5), you will begin to act as Christ directs (Romans 8:5; Galatians 5:22, 23); you will find help in your daily problems and in your praying (Romans 8:26, 27); you will be empowered to serve God and do his will (Acts 1:8; Romans 12:6ff); and you will become part of God's plan to build up his church (Ephesians 4:12, 13).

Christ living in them do not belong to him at all.) ¹⁰And Christ lives within you, so even though your body will die because of sin, the Spirit gives you life* because you have been made right with God. ¹¹The Spirit of God, who raised Jesus from the dead, lives in you. And just as God raised Christ Jesus from the dead, he will give life to your mortal bodies by this same Spirit living within you.

¹²Therefore, dear brothers and sisters,* you have no obligation to do what your sinful nature urges you to do. ¹³For if you live by its dictates, you will die. But if through the power of the Spirit you put to death the deeds of your sinful nature,* you will live. ¹⁴For all who are led by the Spirit of God are children* of God.

¹⁵So you have not received a spirit that makes you fearful slaves. Instead, you received God's Spirit when he adopted you as his own children.* Now we call him, "Abba, Father."* ¹⁶For his Spirit joins with our spirit to affirm that we are God's children. ¹⁷And since we are his children, we are his heirs. In fact, together with Christ we are heirs of God's glory. But if we are to share his glory, we must also share his suffering.

The Future Glory

¹⁸Yet what we suffer now is nothing compared to the glory he will reveal to us later. ¹⁹For all creation is waiting eagerly for that future day when God will reveal who his children really are. ²⁰Against its will, all creation was subjected to God's curse. But with eager hope, ²¹the creation looks forward to the day when it will join God's children in glorious freedom from death and decay. ²²For we know that all creation has been groaning as in the pains of childbirth right up to the present time. ²³And we believers also groan, even though we have the Holy Spirit within us as a foretaste of future glory, for we long for our bodies to be released from sin and suffering. We, too, wait with eager hope for the day when God will give us our full rights as his adopted children,* including the new bodies he has promised us. ²⁴We were given this hope when we were saved. (If we already have something, we don't need to hope* for it. ²⁵But if we look forward to something we don't yet have, we must wait patiently and confidently.)

8:10 Or *your spirit is alive.* **8:12** Greek *brothers;* also in 8:29. **8:13** Greek *deeds of the body.* **8:14** Greek *sons;* also in 8:19. **8:15a** Greek *you received a spirit of sonship.* **8:15b** *Abba* is an Aramaic term for "father." **8:23** Greek *wait anxiously for sonship.* **8:24** Some manuscripts read *wait.*

8:10
John 14:20; 15:5;
17:23, 26
2 Cor 13:5
Col 1:26-27

8:11
Rom 6:5
1 Cor 6:14; 15:45

8:13
Gal 6:8
Col 3:5

8:14
John 1:12
Gal 3:26
Rev 21:7

8:15
Gal 4:5-6

8:16
2 Cor 1:22
Eph 1:13

8:17
Gal 3:29; 4:7

8:18
2 Cor 4:17
Col 3:4
1 Pet 1:6-7

8:19
2 Pet 3:13
1 Jn 3:2

8:20
Gen 3:17-19

8:21
Acts 3:21
2 Pet 3:13
Rev 21:1

8:22
Jer 12:4

8:23
2 Cor 1:22; 5:5
Phil 3:21

8:11 The Holy Spirit is God's promise or guarantee of eternal life for those who believe in him. The Spirit is within us now by faith, and by faith we are certain to live with Christ forever. See Romans 8:23; 1 Corinthians 6:14; 2 Corinthians 4:14; 1 Thessalonians 4:14.

8:13 When we turn away from sin's appeal in the Holy Spirit's power, regarding sin as dead, we can ignore temptation when it comes (see 6:11; Galatians 5:24).

• **8:14-17** Paul uses adoption to illustrate the believer's new relationship with God. In Roman culture, the adopted person lost all rights in his old family and gained all the rights of a legitimate child in his new family. He became a full heir to his new father's estate. Likewise, when a person becomes a Christian, he or she gains all the privileges and responsibilities of a child in God's family. One of these outstanding privileges is being led by the Spirit (see Galatians 4:5, 6). We may not always feel as though we belong to God, but the Holy Spirit is our witness. His inward presence reminds us of who we are and encourages us with God's love (5:5).

• **8:14-17** We are no longer like "fearful slaves"; instead, we are the Master's children. What a privilege! Because we are God's children, we share in great treasures as co-heirs. God has already given us his best gifts: his Son, his Holy Spirit, forgiveness, and eternal life; and he encourages us to ask him for whatever we need.

• **8:17** There is a price for being identified with Jesus. Along with being "heirs of God's glory," Paul also mentions the suffering that Christians must face. What kinds of suffering are we to endure? For first-century believers, there was economic and social persecution, and some even faced death. We, too, must pay a price for following Jesus. In many parts of today's world, Christians face pressures just as severe as those faced by Christ's first followers. Even in countries where Christianity is tolerated or encouraged, Christians must not become complacent. To live as Jesus did—serving others, giving up one's rights, resisting pressures to conform

to the world—always exacts a price. Nothing we suffer, however, can compare to the great price that Jesus paid to save us.

8:19-22 Sin has caused all creation to fall from the perfect state in which God created it. The world is in bondage to death and decay so that it cannot fulfill its intended purpose. One day all creation will be liberated and transformed. Until that time it waits in eager expectation for the resurrection of God's children.

8:19-22 Christians see the world as it is—physically decaying and spiritually infected with sin. But Christians do not need to be pessimistic, because they have hope for future glory. They look forward to the new heaven and new earth that God has promised, and they wait for God's new order that will free the world from sin, sickness, and evil. In the meantime, Christians go with Christ into the world where they heal people's bodies and souls and fight the evil effects of sin in the world.

8:23 We will be resurrected with glorified bodies like the body Christ now has in heaven (see 1 Corinthians 15:25-58). We have the "foretaste," the first installment or down payment of future glory—the Holy Spirit—as a guarantee of our resurrection life (see 2 Corinthians 1:22; 5:5; Ephesians 1:14).

• **8:24, 25** It is natural for children to trust their parents, even though parents sometimes fail to keep their promises. Our heavenly Father, however, never makes promises he won't keep. Nevertheless his plan may take more time than we expect. What are we waiting for? New bodies, a new heaven and new earth, rest and rewards, our eternal family and home, the absence of sin and suffering, and being face to face with Jesus! Rather than acting like impatient children as we wait for God's will to unfold, we need to have confidence in God's perfect timing and wisdom.

8:24, 25 In Romans, Paul presents the idea that salvation is past, present, and future. It is past because we *were* saved the moment we believed in Jesus Christ as Savior (3:21-26; 5:1-11; 6:1-11, 22,

8:26
John 14:16

8:27
1 Cor 4:5

8:28
Eph 1:11; 3:11
2 Tim 1:9

8:29
Eph 1:5
Col 1:18
2 Tim 2:19
Heb 1:6
1 Pet 1:2

8:31
Ps 118:6

8:32
John 3:16
Rom 4:25; 5:8

8:33
Isa 50:8

8:34
Ps 110:1
1 Jn 2:1

8:35
1 Cor 4:11
2 Cor 11:26-27

8:36
†Ps 44:22

8:37
John 16:33
1 Cor 15:57
1 Jn 5:4

26And the Holy Spirit helps us in our weakness. For example, we don't know what God wants us to pray for. But the Holy Spirit prays for us with groanings that cannot be expressed in words. 27And the Father who knows all hearts knows what the Spirit is saying, for the Spirit pleads for us believers* in harmony with God's own will. 28And we know that God causes everything to work together* for the good of those who love God and are called according to his purpose for them. 29For God knew his people in advance, and he chose them to become like his Son, so that his Son would be the firstborn* among many brothers and sisters. 30And having chosen them, he called them to come to him. And having called them, he gave them right standing with himself. And having given them right standing, he gave them his glory.

Nothing Can Separate Us from God's Love

31What shall we say about such wonderful things as these? If God is for us, who can ever be against us? 32Since he did not spare even his own Son but gave him up for us all, won't he also give us everything else? 33Who dares accuse us whom God has chosen for his own? No one—for God himself has given us right standing with himself. 34Who then will condemn us? No one—for Christ Jesus died for us and was raised to life for us, and he is sitting in the place of honor at God's right hand, pleading for us.

35Can anything ever separate us from Christ's love? Does it mean he no longer loves us if we have trouble or calamity, or are persecuted, or hungry, or destitute, or in danger, or threatened with death? 36(As the Scriptures say, "For your sake we are killed every day; we are being slaughtered like sheep."*) 37No, despite all these things, overwhelming victory is ours through Christ, who loved us.

8:27 Greek *for God's holy people.*   **8:28** Some manuscripts read *And we know that everything works together.*
8:29 Or *would be supreme.*   **8:36** Ps 44:22.

23); our new life (eternal life) begins at that moment. And it is present because we *are being* saved; this is the process of sanctification (see the note on 6:1–8:39). But at the same time, we have not fully received all the benefits and blessings of salvation that will be ours when Christ's new Kingdom is completely established. That's our future salvation. While we can be confident of our salvation, we still look ahead with hope and trust toward that complete change of body and personality that lies beyond this life, when we will be like Christ (1 John 3:2).

- **8:26, 27** As a believer, you are not left to your own resources to cope with problems. Even when you don't know the right words to pray, the Holy Spirit prays with and for you, and God answers. With God helping you pray, you don't need to be afraid to come before him. Ask the Holy Spirit to intercede for you "in harmony with God's own will." Then, when you bring your requests to God, trust that he will always do what is best.

- **8:28** God works in "everything"—not just isolated incidents—for our good. This does not mean that all that happens to us is good. Evil is prevalent in our fallen world, but God is able to turn every circumstance around for our long-range good. Note that God is not working to make us happy but to fulfill his purpose. Note also that this promise is not for everybody. It can be claimed only by those who love God and are called by him, that is, those whom the Holy Spirit convinces to receive Christ. Such people have a new perspective, a new mind-set. They trust in God, not in worldly treasures; their security is in heaven, not on earth. Their faith in God does not waver in pain and persecution because they know God is with them.

- **8:29** God's ultimate goal for us is to make us like Christ (1 John 3:2). As we become more and more like him, we discover our true selves, the persons we were created to be. How can we become like Christ? By reading and heeding the Word, by studying his life on earth through the Gospels, by spending time in prayer, by being filled with his Spirit, and by doing his work in the world.

8:29, 30 Some believe these verses mean that before the beginning of the world, God chose certain people to receive his gift of salvation. They point to verses such as Ephesians 1:11, which says that God "chose us in advance, and he makes everything work out according to his plan." Others believe that God knew in advance who would respond to him, and upon those he set his mark (he

chose them). What is clear is that God's *purpose* for people was not an afterthought; it was settled before the foundation of the world. People are to serve and honor God. If you believe in Christ, you can rejoice in the fact that God has always known you. God's love is eternal. His wisdom and power are supreme. He will guide and protect you until you one day stand in his presence.

8:30 *Called* means "summoned or invited." For more on "right standing" (also called justification) and receiving his glory, see the chart in chapter 3, p. 1899.

- **8:31-34** Do you ever think that because you aren't good enough for God, he will not save you? Do you ever feel as if salvation is for everyone else but you? Then these verses are especially for you. If God gave his Son for you, he isn't going to hold back the gift of salvation! If Christ gave his life for you, he isn't going to turn around and condemn you! He will not withhold anything you need to live for him. The book of Romans is more than a theological explanation of God's redeeming grace—it is a letter of comfort and confidence addressed to you.

8:34 Paul says that Jesus is pleading for us in heaven. God has acquitted us and has removed our sin and guilt, so it is Satan, not God, who accuses us. When he does, Jesus, our advocate, sits at God's right hand to present our case. For more on the concept of Christ as our advocate, see the notes on Hebrews 4:14; 4:15.

- **8:35, 36** These words were written to a church that would soon undergo terrible persecution. In just a few years, Paul's hypothetical situations would turn into painful realities. This passage reaffirms God's profound love for his people. No matter what happens to us, no matter where we are, we can never be separated from his love. Suffering should not drive us away from God but help us to identify with him and allow his love to heal us.

- **8:35-39** These verses contain one of the most comforting promises in all Scripture. Believers have always had to face hardships in many forms: persecution, illness, imprisonment, and even death. These sometimes cause them to fear that they have been abandoned by Christ. But Paul exclaims that it is *impossible* to be separated from Christ. His death for us is proof of his unconquerable love. Nothing can separate us from Christ's presence. God tells us how great his love is so that we will feel totally secure in him. If we believe these overwhelming assurances, we will not be afraid.

³⁸And I am convinced that nothing can ever separate us from God's love. Neither death nor life, neither angels nor demons,* neither our fears for today nor our worries about tomorrow—not even the powers of hell can separate us from God's love. ³⁹No power in the sky above or in the earth below—indeed, nothing in all creation will ever be able to separate us from the love of God that is revealed in Christ Jesus our Lord.

8:38
John 10:28
Col 3:3

8:39
Rom 5:3-8

4. Israel's past, present, and future

God's Selection of Israel

9 With Christ as my witness, I speak with utter truthfulness. My conscience and the Holy Spirit confirm it. ²My heart is filled with bitter sorrow and unending grief ³for my people, my Jewish brothers and sisters.* I would be willing to be forever cursed—cut off from Christ!—if that would save them. ⁴They are the people of Israel, chosen to be God's adopted children.* God revealed his glory to them. He made covenants with them and gave them his law. He gave them the privilege of worshiping him and receiving his wonderful promises. ⁵Abraham, Isaac, and Jacob are their ancestors, and Christ himself was an Israelite as far as his human nature is concerned. And he is God, the one who rules over everything and is worthy of eternal praise! Amen.*

9:1
1 Tim 2:7

9:3
Exod 32:32

9:4
Exod 4:22
Deut 4:13; 7:6
Eph 2:12

9:5
John 1:1, 18
Rom 1:3
Titus 2:13
2 Pet 1:1
1 Jn 5:20

⁶Well then, has God failed to fulfill his promise to Israel? No, for not all who are born into the nation of Israel are truly members of God's people! ⁷Being descendants of Abraham doesn't make them truly Abraham's children. For the Scriptures say, "Isaac is the son through whom your descendants will be counted,"* though Abraham had other children, too. ⁸This means that Abraham's physical descendants are not necessarily children of God. Only the children of the promise are considered to be Abraham's children. ⁹For God had promised, "I will return about this time next year, and Sarah will have a son."*

9:6
Num 23:19
Rom 2:28
Gal 6:16

9:7
†Gen 21:12
Heb 11:18

9:8
Rom 8:14
Gal 3:16; 4:23

9:9
†Gen 18:10, 14

¹⁰This son was our ancestor Isaac. When he married Rebekah, she gave birth to twins.* ¹¹But before they were born, before they had done anything good or bad, she received a message from God. (This message shows that God chooses people according to his own purposes; ¹²he calls people, but not according to their good or bad works.) She was told, "Your older son will serve your younger son."* ¹³In the words of the Scriptures, "I loved Jacob, but I rejected Esau."*

9:10
Gen 25:21

9:12
†Gen 25:23

9:13
†Mal 1:2-3

¹⁴Are we saying, then, that God was unfair? Of course not! ¹⁵For God said to Moses,

9:14
Deut 32:4

> "I will show mercy to anyone I choose,
>   and I will show compassion to anyone I choose."*

9:15
†Exod 33:19

¹⁶So it is God who decides to show mercy. We can neither choose it nor work for it.

9:16
Eph 2:8

8:38 Greek *nor rulers.* **9:3** Greek *my brothers.* **9:4** Greek *chosen for sonship.* **9:5** Or *May God, the one who rules over everything, be praised forever. Amen.* **9:7** Gen 21:12. **9:9** Gen 18:10, 14. **9:10** Greek *she conceived children through this one man.* **9:12** Gen 25:23. **9:13** Mal 1:2-3. **9:15** Exod 33:19.

8:38 *Powers* are unseen forces of evil in the universe, forces like Satan and his fallen angels (see Ephesians 6:12). In Christ we are super-conquerors, and his love will protect us from any such forces.

• **9:1-3** Paul expressed concern for his Jewish brothers and sisters by saying that he would willingly take their punishment if that would save them. While the only one who can save us is Christ, Paul showed a rare depth of love. Like Jesus, he was willing to sacrifice so others would be saved. How concerned are you for those who don't know Christ? Are you willing to sacrifice your time, money, energy, comfort, and safety to see them come to faith in Jesus?

9:4 The Jews viewed God's choosing of Israel in the Old Testament as being like adoption. They were undeserving and without rights as natural children. Yet God adopted them and granted them the status of his sons and daughters.

9:6 God's word in the form of beautiful covenant promises came to Abraham. Covenant people, the true children of Abraham, are not just his biological descendants. They are all those who trust in God and in what Jesus Christ has done for them (see also 2:29; Galatians 3:7).

9:11 The Jews were proud of the fact that their lineage came from Isaac, whose mother was Sarah (Abraham's legitimate wife), rather than Ishmael, whose mother was Hagar (Sarah's

servant). Paul asserts that no one can claim to be chosen by God because of his or her heritage or good deeds. God freely chooses to save whomever he wills. The doctrine of election teaches that it is God's sovereign choice to save us by his goodness and mercy, not by our own merit.

9:12-14 Was it right for God to choose Jacob, the younger, to be over Esau? In Malachi 1:2, 3, the statement "This is how I showed my love for you: I loved your ancestor Jacob, but I rejected his brother Esau" refers to the nations of Israel and Edom rather than to the individual brothers. God chose Jacob to continue the family line of the faithful because he knew his heart was for God. But he did not exclude Esau from knowing and loving him. Keep in mind the kind of God we worship: He is sovereign; he is not arbitrary; in all things he works for our good; he is trustworthy; he will save all who believe in him. When we understand these qualities of God, we know that his choices are good even if we don't understand all his reasons.

9:16 The fallacy of gaining salvation by human effort remains as strong as ever—people still think good intentions are the key to unlock the door to eternal life. By the time they get to try the lock, they will find that their key does not fit. Others imagine that their efforts are building an invisible ladder to heaven made up of service, family, position, reputation, good work, and desire, although none of these rungs will support a feather. People are so busy trying to reach God that they completely miss the truth

9:17
†Exod 9:16
9:18
Exod 4:21; 14:4
Josh 11:20
Rom 11:25

17For the Scriptures say that God told Pharaoh, "I have appointed you for the very purpose of displaying my power in you and to spread my fame throughout the earth."* 18So you see, God chooses to show mercy to some, and he chooses to harden the hearts of others so they refuse to listen.

19Well then, you might say, "Why does God blame people for not responding? Haven't they simply done what he makes them do?"

9:20
Isa 29:16; 45:9

20No, don't say that. Who are you, a mere human being, to argue with God? Should the thing that was created say to the one who created it, "Why have you made me like this?"

9:21
Jer 18:6
2 Tim 2:20
9:22
Jer 50:25
9:23
Rom 8:30
9:24
Rom 3:29

21When a potter makes jars out of clay, doesn't he have a right to use the same lump of clay to make one jar for decoration and another to throw garbage into? 22In the same way, even though God has the right to show his anger and his power, he is very patient with those on whom his anger falls, who are destined for destruction. 23He does this to make the riches of his glory shine even brighter on those to whom he shows mercy, who were prepared in advance for glory. 24And we are among those whom he selected, both from the Jews and from the Gentiles.

9:25
†Hos 2:23

25Concerning the Gentiles, God says in the prophecy of Hosea,

> "Those who were not my people,
>   I will now call my people.
> And I will love those
>   whom I did not love before."*

9:26
†Hos 1:10

26And,

> "Then, at the place where they were told,
>   'You are not my people,'
> there they will be called
>   'children of the living God.'"*

9:17 Exod 9:16 (Greek version).   **9:25** Hos 2:23.   **9:26** Greek *sons of the living God.* Hos 1:10.

WARNING SIGNS OF DEVELOPING HARDNESS

Hardening is like a callus or like the tough bone fibers that bridge a fracture. Spiritual hardening begins with self-sufficiency, security in one's self, and self-satisfaction. The real danger is that at some point, repeated resistance to God will yield an actual inability to respond, which the Bible describes as a hardened heart. Insensitivity indicates advanced hardening. Here are some of the warning signs:

Warning Sign	Reference
Disobeying—Pharaoh's willful disobedience led to his hardened heart.	Exodus 4:21
Having wealth and prosperity—Taking God's blessings for granted can cause us to feel as if they were owed to us.	Deuteronomy 8:6-14
Rebelling and being discontented—Suffering or discomfort can create an attitude that blames God.	Psalm 95:8
Rejecting a deserved rebuke—Rejecting God's gift makes our neck stiff and our heart hard.	Proverbs 29:1
Refusing to listen—Refusing to listen leads to a loss of spiritual hearing.	Zechariah 7:11-13
Failing to respond—Listening to God with no intention of obeying produces an inability to obey.	Matthew 13:11-15

---

that God has already reached down to them. We cannot earn God's mercy—if we could, it would not be mercy.

9:17, 18 Paul quotes from Exodus 9:16, where God foretold how Pharaoh would be used to declare God's power. Paul uses this argument to show that salvation was God's work, not people's. God's judgment on Pharaoh's choice to resist God was to confirm that sin and harden his heart. The consequences of Pharaoh's rebellion would be his own punishment.

• **9:21** With this illustration, Paul is not saying that some of us are worth more than others but that the Creator has control over the created object. The created object, therefore, has no right to demand anything from its Creator—its very existence depends

on him. Keeping this perspective removes any temptation to have pride in personal achievement.

9:25, 26 About seven hundred years before Jesus' birth, Hosea told of God's intention to restore his people. Paul applies Hosea's message to God's intention to bring Gentiles into his family after the Jews rejected his plan. Verse 25 is a quotation from Hosea 2:23 and verse 26 is from Hosea 1:10.

27And concerning Israel, Isaiah the prophet cried out,

"Though the people of Israel are as numerous as the sand of the seashore,
only a remnant will be saved.
28 For the LORD will carry out his sentence upon the earth
quickly and with finality."*

29And Isaiah said the same thing in another place:

"If the LORD of Heaven's Armies
had not spared a few of our children,
we would have been wiped out like Sodom,
destroyed like Gomorrah."*

Israel's Unbelief

30What does all this mean? Even though the Gentiles were not trying to follow God's standards, they were made right with God. And it was by faith that this took place. 31But the people of Israel, who tried so hard to get right with God by keeping the law, never succeeded. 32Why not? Because they were trying to get right with God by keeping the law* instead of by trusting in him. They stumbled over the great rock in their path. 33God warned them of this in the Scriptures when he said,

"I am placing a stone in Jerusalem* that makes people stumble,
a rock that makes them fall.
But anyone who trusts in him
will never be disgraced."*

10 Dear brothers and sisters,* the longing of my heart and my prayer to God is for the people of Israel to be saved. 2I know what enthusiasm they have for God, but it is misdirected zeal. 3For they don't understand God's way of making people right with himself. Refusing to accept God's way, they cling to their own way of getting right with God by trying to keep the law. 4For Christ has already accomplished the purpose for which the law was given.* As a result, all who believe in him are made right with God.

9:27
†Isa 10:22
†Hos 1:10

9:28
†Isa 10:22-23;
28:22

9:29
†Isa 1:9

9:30
Gal 2:16
Heb 11:7

9:31
Isa 51:1
Rom 10:2-3
Gal 5:4

9:33
Rom 10:11
1 Pet 2:6, 8

10:2
Acts 22:3

10:3
Rom 9:31-32

10:4
Gal 3:24

9:27-28 Isa 10:22-23 (Greek version). **9:29** Isa 1:9. **9:32** Greek *by works*. **9:33a** Greek *in Zion*. **9:33b** Isa 8:14;
28:16 (Greek version). **10:1** Greek *Brothers*. **10:4** Or *For Christ is the end of the law.*

9:27-29 Isaiah prophesied that only a small number of God's original people, the Jews, would be saved. Paul saw this happening in every city where he preached. Even though he went to the Jews first, relatively few ever accepted the message. Verses 27 and 28 are based on Isaiah 10:22, 23; and 9:29 is from Isaiah 1:9.

• **9:31-33** Sometimes we are like these people, trying to get right with God by keeping his laws. We may think that attending church, doing church work, giving offerings, and being nice will be enough. After all, we've played by the rules, haven't we? But Paul's words sting—this approach never succeeds. Paul explains that God's plan is not for those who try to earn his favor by being good; it is for those who realize that they can never be good enough and so must depend on Christ. We can be saved only by putting our faith in what Jesus Christ has done. If we do that, we will never be disappointed.

• **9:32** The Jews had a worthy goal—to honor God. But they tried to achieve it the wrong way—by rigid and painstaking obedience to the law. Thus, some of them became more dedicated to the law than to God. They thought that if they kept the law, God would have to accept them as his people. But God cannot be controlled. The Jews did not see that their Scriptures, the Old Testament, taught that salvation depended on faith, not on human effort (see Genesis 15:6).

• **9:32** The "great rock" they stumbled over was Jesus. The Jews did not believe in him because he didn't meet their expectations for the Messiah. Some people still stumble over Christ because salvation by faith doesn't make sense to them. They think they

must earn their way to God, or perhaps God will simply overlook their sins. Others stumble over Christ because his values are the opposite of the world's. He asks for humility, and many are unwilling to humble themselves before him. He requires obedience, and many refuse to put their wills at his disposal. Have you stumbled over this rock, or have you chosen to build your life on it?

10:1 What will happen to the Jewish people who believe in God but not in Christ? Since they believe in the same God, won't they be saved? If that were true, Paul would not have worked so hard and sacrificed so much to teach them about Christ. Because Jesus is the most complete revelation of God, we cannot fully know God apart from Christ; and because God appointed Jesus to bring God and people together, we cannot come to God by another way. The Jews, like everyone else, must find salvation through Jesus Christ (John 14:6; Acts 4:12). Like Paul, we should pray that all Jews might be saved and lovingly share the Good News with them.

• **10:3-5** Rather than living by faith in God, the Jews established customs and traditions (in addition to God's law) to try to make themselves acceptable in God's sight. But human effort, no matter how sincere, can never substitute for the righteousness God offers us by faith. The only way to *earn* salvation is to be perfect—and that is impossible. We can only hold out our empty hands and receive salvation as a gift.

10:4 Christ accomplished the purpose for which the law was given in two ways: He fulfills the purpose and goal of the law (Matthew 5:17) in that he perfectly exemplified God's desires on earth. But he is also the termination of the law because in comparison to Christ, the law is powerless to save.

Salvation Is for Everyone

10:5
Lev 18:5
Ezek 20:11, 13, 21
Rom 7:10

10:6-8
†Deut 30:12-14

⁵For Moses writes that the law's way of making a person right with God requires obedience to all of its commands.* ⁶But faith's way of getting right with God says, "Don't say in your heart,'Who will go up to heaven?' (to bring Christ down to earth). ⁷And don't say,'Who will go down to the place of the dead?' (to bring Christ back to life again)." ⁸In fact, it says,

> "The message is very close at hand;
>   it is on your lips and in your heart."*

10:9
Matt 10:32

10:11
†Isa 28:16
Rom 9:33

10:12
Acts 15:9
Eph 2:4-7

10:13
†Joel 2:32
Acts 2:21

10:15
†Isa 52:7
†Nah 1:15

And that message is the very message about faith that we preach: ⁹If you confess with your mouth that Jesus is Lord and believe in your heart that God raised him from the dead, you will be saved. ¹⁰For it is by believing in your heart that you are made right with God, and it is by confessing with your mouth that you are saved. ¹¹As the Scriptures tell us, "Anyone who trusts in him will never be disgraced."* ¹²Jew and Gentile* are the same in this respect. They have the same Lord, who gives generously to all who call on him. ¹³For "Everyone who calls on the name of the LORD will be saved."*

¹⁴But how can they call on him to save them unless they believe in him? And how can they believe in him if they have never heard about him? And how can they hear about him unless someone tells them? ¹⁵And how will anyone go and tell them without being sent? That is why the Scriptures say, "How beautiful are the feet of messengers who bring good news!"*

10:16
†Isa 53:1
John 12:38
Heb 4:2

10:17
Gal 3:2, 5
Col 3:16

10:18
†Ps 19:4

¹⁶But not everyone welcomes the Good News, for Isaiah the prophet said, "LORD, who has believed our message?"* ¹⁷So faith comes from hearing, that is, hearing the Good News about Christ. ¹⁸But I ask, have the people of Israel actually heard the message? Yes, they have:

> "The message has gone throughout the earth,
>   and the words to all the world."*

10:19
†Deut 32:21

¹⁹But I ask, did the people of Israel really understand? Yes, they did, for even in the time of Moses, God said,

> "I will rouse your jealousy through people who are not even a nation.
>   I will provoke your anger through the foolish Gentiles."*

10:20
†Isa 65:1
Rom 9:30

²⁰And later Isaiah spoke boldly for God, saying,

> "I was found by people who were not looking for me.
>   I showed myself to those who were not asking for me."*

10:5 See Lev 18:5.   **10:6-8** Deut 30:12-14.   **10:11** Isa 28:16 (Greek version).   **10:12** Greek *and Greek.*
10:13 Joel 2:32.   **10:15** Isa 52:7.   **10:16** Isa 53:1.   **10:18** Ps 19:4.   **10:19** Deut 32:21.   **10:20** Isa 65:1
(Greek version).

10:5 In order to be saved by the law, a person would have to live a perfect life, not sinning once. Then why did God give the law since he knew people couldn't keep it? According to Paul, one reason the law was given was to show people how guilty they are (Galatians 3:19). The law was a shadow of Christ—that is, the sacrificial system educated the people so that when the true sacrifice came, they would be able to understand his work (Hebrews 10:1-4). The system of ceremonial laws was to last until the coming of Christ. The law points to our need for a Savior.

10:6-8 Paul adapts Moses' farewell challenge from Deuteronomy 30:11-14 to apply to Christ. Christ has provided our salvation through his incarnation (God in human form) and resurrection. God's salvation is right in front of us. He will come to us wherever we are. All we need to do is to respond and accept his gift of salvation.

• **10:8-12** Have you ever been asked, "How do I become a Christian?" These verses give you the beautiful answer: Salvation is as close as your own lips and heart. People think it must be a complicated process, but it is not. If we believe in our heart and say with our mouth that Christ is the risen Lord, we will be saved.

• **10:14** In telling others about Christ, an effective witness must include more than being a good example. Eventually, we will have to explain the content, the *what* and the *how* of the gospel. Modeling the Christian life is important, but we will need to

connect the mind of the unbeliever and the message of the gospel. There should never be a debate between those who favor life-style evangelism (one's living proclaims the gospel) and confrontational evangelism (declaring the message). Both should be used together in promoting the gospel.

• **10:15** We must take God's great message of salvation to others so that they can respond to the Good News. How will your loved ones and neighbors hear it unless someone tells them? Is God calling you to take a part in making his message known in your community? Think of one person who needs to hear the Good News, and think of something you can do to help him or her hear it. Then take that step as soon as possible.

• **10:18-20** Many Jews who looked for the Messiah refused to believe in him when he came. God offered his salvation to the Gentiles ("people who were not looking for me"); thus, many Gentiles who didn't even know about a Messiah found and believed in him. Some religious people are spiritually blind, while those who have never been in a church are sometimes the most responsive to God's message. Because appearances are deceiving, and we can't see into people's hearts, beware of judging beforehand who will respond to the Good News and who will not.

²¹But regarding Israel, God said,

> "All day long I opened my arms to them,
>   but they were disobedient and rebellious."*

10:21
†Isa 65:2

God's Mercy on Israel

11 I ask, then, has God rejected his own people, the nation of Israel? Of course not! I myself am an Israelite, a descendant of Abraham and a member of the tribe of Benjamin. ²No, God has not rejected his own people, whom he chose from the very beginning. Do you realize what the Scriptures say about this? Elijah the prophet complained to God about the people of Israel and said, ³"LORD, they have killed your prophets and torn down your altars. I am the only one left, and now they are trying to kill me, too."*

⁴And do you remember God's reply? He said, "No, I have 7,000 others who have never bowed down to Baal!"*

⁵It is the same today, for a few of the people of Israel* have remained faithful because of God's grace—his undeserved kindness in choosing them. ⁶And since it is through God's kindness, then it is not by their good works. For in that case, God's grace would not be what it really is—free and undeserved.

⁷So this is the situation: Most of the people of Israel have not found the favor of God they are looking for so earnestly. A few have—the ones God has chosen—but the hearts of the rest were hardened. ⁸As the Scriptures say,

> "God has put them into a deep sleep.
> To this day he has shut their eyes so they do not see,
>   and closed their ears so they do not hear."*

⁹Likewise, David said,

> "Let their bountiful table become a snare,
>   a trap that makes them think all is well.
> Let their blessings cause them to stumble,
>   and let them get what they deserve.
> ¹⁰ Let their eyes go blind so they cannot see,
>   and let their backs be bent forever."*

11:1
Phil 3:5

11:2
1 Sam 12:22

11:3
†1 Kgs 19:10, 14

11:4
†1 Kgs 19:18

11:5
Rom 9:27

11:6
Rom 4:4

11:7
Rom 9:31

11:8
†Deut 29:4
†Isa 29:10
Matt 13:14
John 12:40
Acts 28:26-27

11:9-10
†Ps 69:22-23

¹¹Did God's people stumble and fall beyond recovery? Of course not! They were disobedient, so God made salvation available to the Gentiles. But he wanted his own people to become jealous and claim it for themselves. ¹²Now if the Gentiles were enriched because the people of Israel turned down God's offer of salvation, think how much greater a blessing the world will share when they finally accept it.

11:11
Acts 13:46; 18:6

10:21 Isa 65:2 (Greek version).   11:3 1 Kgs 19:10, 14.   11:4 1 Kgs 19:18.   11:5 Greek *for a remnant.*   11:8 Isa 29:10; Deut 29:4.   11:9-10 Ps 69:22-23 (Greek version).

11:1ff In this chapter Paul points out that not *all* Jews have rejected God's message of salvation. There are still a faithful few (11:5). Paul himself, after all, was a Jew, and so were Jesus' disciples and nearly all of the early Christian missionaries.

11:2 Elijah was a great reforming prophet who challenged the northern kingdom of Israel to repent. See his Profile in 1 Kings 17, p. 545 for more information.

• **11:2** God chose the Jews ("his own people") to be the people through whom the rest of the world could find salvation. But this did not mean the entire Jewish nation would be saved; only those who were faithful to God were considered true Jews (11:5). We are saved through faith in Christ, not because we are part of a nation, religion, or family. On whom or on what are you depending for salvation?

• **11:6** Do you think it's easier for God to love you when you're good? Do you secretly suspect that God chose you because you deserved it? Do you think some people's behavior is so bad that God couldn't possibly save them? If you ever think this way, you don't entirely understand that salvation is by grace, a free gift. It cannot be earned, in whole or in part; it can only be accepted with thankfulness and praise.

11:7 "The hearts of the rest were hardened" was God's punishment for their sin. It was a confirmation of their own stubbornness.

In judging them, God removed their ability to see and hear and to turn from sin; thus, they would experience the consequences of their rebellion. Resisting God is like saying to him, "Leave me alone!" But because God is always and everywhere present, his answer to that prayer might be to agree and make that person less sensitive, more hardened to him. The very possibility of that happening ought to keep us asking God specifically for ears that really hear and eyes that really see—openness and responsiveness to him.

11:8-10 These verses describe the punishment for unresponsive hearts predicted by the prophet Isaiah (Isaiah 6:9-13). If people refuse to hear God's Good News, they eventually will be unable to understand it. Paul saw this happening in the Jewish congregations he visited on his missionary journeys. (Verse 8 is based on Deuteronomy 29:4 and Isaiah 29:10. Verses 9 and 10 are from Psalm 69:22, 23.)

11:11ff Paul had a vision of a church where all Jewish and Gentile believers would be united in their love of God and in obedience to Christ. While respecting God's law, this ideal church would look to Christ alone for salvation. A person's ethnic background and social status would be irrelevant (see Galatians 3:28). What mattered would be his or her faith in Christ.

But Paul's vision has not yet been realized. For the most part, Jewish people have rejected the Good News. They have depended

¹³I am saying all this especially for you Gentiles. God has appointed me as the apostle to the Gentiles. I stress this, ¹⁴for I want somehow to make the people of Israel jealous of what you Gentiles have, so I might save some of them. ¹⁵For since their rejection meant that God offered salvation to the rest of the world, their acceptance will be even more wonderful. It will be life for those who were dead! ¹⁶And since Abraham and the other patriarchs were holy, their descendants will also be holy—just as the entire batch of dough is holy because the portion given as an offering is holy. For if the roots of the tree are holy, the branches will be, too.

¹⁷But some of these branches from Abraham's tree—some of the people of Israel—have been broken off. And you Gentiles, who were branches from a wild olive tree, have been grafted in. So now you also receive the blessing God has promised Abraham and his children, sharing in the rich nourishment from the root of God's special olive tree. ¹⁸But you must not brag about being grafted in to replace the branches that were broken off. You are just a branch, not the root.

¹⁹"Well," you may say, "those branches were broken off to make room for me." ²⁰Yes, but remember—those branches were broken off because they didn't believe in Christ, and you are there because you do believe. So don't think highly of yourself, but fear what could happen. ²¹For if God did not spare the original branches, he won't* spare you either.

²²Notice how God is both kind and severe. He is severe toward those who disobeyed, but kind to you if you continue to trust in his kindness. But if you stop trusting, you also will be cut off. ²³And if the people of Israel turn from their unbelief, they will be grafted in again, for God has the power to graft them back into the tree. ²⁴You, by nature, were a branch cut from a wild olive tree. So if God was willing to do something contrary to nature by grafting you into his cultivated tree, he will be far more eager to graft the original branches back into the tree where they belong.

God's Mercy Is for Everyone

²⁵I want you to understand this mystery, dear brothers and sisters,* so that you will not feel proud about yourselves. Some of the people of Israel have hard hearts, but this will last only until the full number of Gentiles comes to Christ. ²⁶And so all Israel will be saved. As the Scriptures say,

"The one who rescues will come from Jerusalem,*
    and he will turn Israel* away from ungodliness.
²⁷ And this is my covenant with them,
    that I will take away their sins."*

11:21 Some manuscripts read *perhaps he won't.* **11:25** Greek *brothers.* **11:26a** Greek *from Zion.*
11:26b Greek *Jacob.* **11:26-27** Isa 59:20-21; 27:9 (Greek version).

Cross references (margin):

11:14
1 Cor 9:20
2 Tim 1:9

11:15
Luke 15:24, 32
Rom 5:10

11:17
Jer 11:16
Eph 2:11-16

11:18
John 4:22

11:20
Rom 12:16

11:22
John 15:2, 14
Heb 3:14

11:23
2 Cor 3:14-16

11:25
Luke 21:24
Rom 12:16

11:26-27
Ps 14:7
†Isa 59:20-21
Jer 31:31-34
Heb 8:8; 10:16

---

on their heritage for salvation, and they do not have the heart of obedience that was so important to the Old Testament prophets and to Paul. Once Gentiles became dominant in many of the Christian churches, they began rejecting Jews and even persecuting them. Unfortunately, this practice has recurred through the centuries.

True Christians should not persecute others. Both Gentiles and Jews have done so much to damage the cause of Christ, whom they claim to serve, that Paul's vision often seems impossible to fulfill. Yet God chose the Jews, just as he chose the Gentiles, and he is still working to unite all believers so they become a holy temple where God lives by his Spirit (see Ephesians 2:11-22).

11:13-15 Paul was appointed as an apostle to the Gentiles. He reminded his Jewish brothers and sisters of this fact, hoping that they, too, would want to be saved. The Jews rejected God's offer, and, thus, Gentiles were being offered salvation. But when a Jew comes to Christ, there is great rejoicing, as if a dead person has come back to life.

• **11:16-24** Speaking to Gentile Christians, Paul warns them not to feel superior because some Jews were rejected. Abraham's faith is like the root of a productive tree, and the Jewish people are the tree's natural branches. Because of faithlessness, some of the Jews have been broken off, and Gentile believers, who were branches from a wild olive tree, have been grafted in. Both Jews and Gentiles share the tree's nourishment based on faith in God; neither can rest on heritage or culture for salvation.

11:22 "Continue to trust in his kindness" refers to steadfast perseverance in faith. Steadfastness is a proof of the reality of faith and a by-product of salvation, not a means to it.

• **11:26** Some say the phrase "and so all Israel will be saved" means that the majority of Jews in the final generation before Christ's return will turn to Christ for salvation. Others say that Paul is using the term *Israel* to refer to the "spiritual" nation of Israel, which is comprised of Jews and Gentiles who have received salvation through faith in Christ. Thus, "all Israel" (or all believers) will receive God's promised gift of salvation. Still others say that "all Israel" means Israel as a whole will have a role in Christ's Kingdom. The Jews' identity as a people won't be discarded. God chose the nation of Israel, and he has never rejected it. He also chose the church, through Jesus Christ, and he will never reject it either. This does not mean, of course, that all Jews or all church members will be saved. It is possible to be Jewish or to belong to a church without ever responding in faith. But just because some people have rejected Christ does not mean that God stops working with either Israel or the church. He continues to offer salvation freely to all. Still others say that the phrase "and so" means "in this way" or "this is how," referring to the necessity of faith in Christ.

28Many of the people of Israel are now enemies of the Good News, and this benefits you Gentiles. Yet they are still the people he loves because he chose their ancestors Abraham, Isaac, and Jacob. 29For God's gifts and his call can never be withdrawn. 30Once, you Gentiles were rebels against God, but when the people of Israel rebelled against him, God was merciful to you instead. 31Now they are the rebels, and God's mercy has come to you so that they, too, will share* in God's mercy. 32For God has imprisoned everyone in disobedience so he could have mercy on everyone.

33Oh, how great are God's riches and wisdom and knowledge! How impossible it is for us to understand his decisions and his ways!

34 For who can know the Lord's thoughts?
　　Who knows enough to give him advice?*
35 And who has given him so much
　　　that he needs to pay it back?*

36For everything comes from him and exists by his power and is intended for his glory. All glory to him forever! Amen.

11:29
Heb 7:21

11:32
Gal 3:22
1 Tim 2:4

11:33
Isa 45:15; 55:8

11:34
Job 15:8; 36:22
†Isa 40:13
Jer 23:18
1 Cor 2:16

11:35
Job 41:11

11:36
1 Cor 8:6

B. HOW TO BEHAVE (12:1—16:27)

Moving from the theological to the practical, Paul gives guidelines for living as a redeemed people in a fallen world. We are to give ourselves to Christ as living sacrifices, obey the government, love our neighbors, and take special care of those who are weak in the faith. He closes with personal remarks. Throughout this section, we learn how to live our faith each day.

1. Personal responsibility

A Living Sacrifice to God

12 And so, dear brothers and sisters,* I plead with you to give your bodies to God because of all he has done for you. Let them be a living and holy sacrifice—the kind he will find acceptable. This is truly the way to worship him.* 2Don't copy the behavior and customs of this world, but let God transform you into a new person by changing the way you think. Then you will learn to know God's will for you, which is good and pleasing and perfect.

3Because of the privilege and authority* God has given me, I give each of you this warning: Don't think you are better than you really are. Be honest in your evaluation of yourselves,

12:1
Rom 6:13
1 Pet 2:5

12:2
Gal 1:4
Eph 4:23
Col 3:10

12:3
1 Cor 12:11
Eph 4:7

11:31 Other manuscripts read *will now share;* still others read *will someday share.* **11:34** Isa 40:13 (Greek version). **11:35** See Job 41:11. **12:1a** Greek *brothers.* **12:1b** Or *This is your spiritual worship;* or *This is your reasonable service.* **12:3a** Or *Because of the grace;* compare 1:5.

11:28-32 In this passage Paul shows how the Jews and the Gentiles benefit each other. Whenever God shows mercy to one group, the other shares the blessing. In God's original plan, the Jews would be the source of God's blessing to the Gentiles (see Genesis 12:3). When the Jews neglected this mission, God blessed the Gentiles anyway through the Jewish Messiah. He still maintained his love for the Jews because of his promises to Abraham, Isaac, and Jacob. The privileges and invitation of God given to Israel will never be withdrawn. But someday all faithful Jews will share in God's mercy. God's plans will not be thwarted: He will "have mercy on everyone." For a beautiful picture of Jews and Gentiles experiencing rich blessings, see Isaiah 60.

11:34-36 The implication of these questions is that no one has fully understood the mind of the Lord. No one has been his counselor. And God owes nothing to any one of us. Isaiah and Jeremiah asked similar questions to show that we are unable to give advice to God or criticize his ways (Isaiah 40:13; Jeremiah 23:18). God alone is the possessor of absolute power and absolute wisdom. In the final analysis, all of us are absolutely dependent on God. He is the source of all things, including ourselves. He is the power that sustains and rules the world that we live in. And God works out all things to bring glory to himself. The all-powerful God deserves our praise.

• **12:1** When sacrificing an animal according to God's law, a priest would kill the animal, cut it in pieces, and place it on the altar. Sacrifice was important, but even in the Old Testament God made it clear that obedience from the heart was much more important (see 1 Samuel 15:22; Psalm 40:6; Amos 5:21-24). God wants us to offer ourselves, not animals, as *living* sacrifices—daily laying

aside our own desires to follow him, putting all our energy and resources at his disposal and trusting him to guide us. We do this out of gratitude that our sins have been forgiven.

• **12:1, 2** God has good, pleasing, and perfect plans for his children. He wants us to be transformed people with renewed minds, living to honor and obey him. Because he wants only what is best for us, and because he gave his Son to make our new life possible, we should joyfully give ourselves as living sacrifices for his service.

• **12:2** Paul warned Christians: "Don't copy the behavior and customs of this world" that are usually selfish and often corrupting. Wise Christians decide that much worldly behavior is off-limits for them. Our refusal to conform to this world's values, however, must go even deeper than just behavior and customs; it must be firmly planted in our mind: "Let God transform you into a new person by changing the way you think." It is possible to avoid most worldly customs and still be proud, covetous, selfish, stubborn, and arrogant. Only when the Holy Spirit renews, reeducates, and redirects our mind are we truly transformed (see 8:5).

• **12:3** Healthy self-esteem is important because some of us think too little of ourselves; on the other hand, some of us overestimate ourselves. The key to an honest and accurate self-evaluation is knowing the basis of our self-worth—our identity in Christ. Apart from him, we aren't capable of very much by eternal standards; in him, we are valuable and capable of worthy service. Evaluating yourself by the worldly standards of success and achievement can cause you to think too much about your worth in the eyes of others and thus miss your true value in God's eyes.

12:4
1 Cor 12:12

12:5
Eph 4:25

12:6-8
1 Pet 4:10-11

12:9
Amos 5:15
1 Tim 1:5

12:10
John 13:34
Phil 2:3
1 Thes 4:9
2 Pet 1:7

12:11
Acts 18:25; 20:19
Rev 3:15

12:13
Heb 13:2

12:14
Matt 5:44

12:15
Job 30:25

12:16
Prov 3:7
Isa 5:21

measuring yourselves by the faith God has given us.* ⁴Just as our bodies have many parts and each part has a special function, ⁵so it is with Christ's body. We are many parts of one body, and we all belong to each other.

⁶In his grace, God has given us different gifts for doing certain things well. So if God has given you the ability to prophesy, speak out with as much faith as God has given you. ⁷If your gift is serving others, serve them well. If you are a teacher, teach well. ⁸If your gift is to encourage others, be encouraging. If it is giving, give generously. If God has given you leadership ability, take the responsibility seriously. And if you have a gift for showing kindness to others, do it gladly.

⁹Don't just pretend to love others. Really love them. Hate what is wrong. Hold tightly to what is good. ¹⁰Love each other with genuine affection,* and take delight in honoring each other. ¹¹Never be lazy, but work hard and serve the Lord enthusiastically.* ¹²Rejoice in our confident hope. Be patient in trouble, and keep on praying. ¹³When God's people are in need, be ready to help them. Always be eager to practice hospitality.

¹⁴Bless those who persecute you. Don't curse them; pray that God will bless them. ¹⁵Be happy with those who are happy, and weep with those who weep. ¹⁶Live in harmony with each other. Don't be too proud to enjoy the company of ordinary people. And don't think you know it all!

12:3b Or *by the faith God has given you;* or *by the standard of our God-given faith.*   **12:10** Greek *with brotherly love.*
12:11 Or *but serve the Lord with a zealous spirit;* or *but let the Spirit excite you as you serve the Lord.*

12:4, 5 Paul uses the concept of the human body to teach how Christians should live and work together. Just as the parts of the body function under the direction of the brain, so Christians are to work together under the command and authority of Jesus Christ (see 1 Corinthians 12:12-31; Ephesians 4:1-16).

● **12:6** God gives us gifts so we can build up his church. To use them effectively, we must (1) realize that all gifts and abilities come from God; (2) understand that not everyone has the same gifts; (3) know who we are and what we do best; (4) dedicate our gifts to God's service and not to our personal success; (5) be willing to utilize our gifts wholeheartedly, not holding back anything from God's service. God's gifts differ in nature, power, and effectiveness according to his wisdom and graciousness, not according to our faith. Our role is to be faithful and to seek ways to serve others with what Christ has given us.

12:6 "Prophesying" in Scripture is not always predicting the future. Often it means preaching God's messages (1 Corinthians 14:1-3).

● **12:6-8** Look at this list of gifts and imagine the kinds of people who would have each gift. Prophets are often bold and articulate. Servers (those in ministry) are faithful and loyal. Teachers are clear thinkers. Encouragers know how to motivate others. Givers are generous and trusting. Leaders are good organizers and managers. Those who show kindness are caring people who are happy to give their time to others. It would be difficult for one person to embody all these gifts. An assertive prophet would not usually make a good counselor, and a generous giver might fail as a leader. When you identify your own gifts (and this list is far from complete), ask how you can use them to build up God's family. At the same time, realize that your gifts can't do the work of the church all alone. Be thankful for people whose gifts are completely different from yours. Let your strengths balance their weaknesses, and be grateful that their abilities make up for your deficiencies. Together you can build Christ's church.

● **12:9-10** Most of us have learned how to be courteous to others—how to speak kindly, avoid hurting their feelings, and appear to take an interest in them. We may even be skilled in pretending to show compassion when we hear of others' needs, or to become indignant when we learn of injustice. But God calls us to real and genuine love that goes far beyond being hypocritical and polite. Genuine love requires concentration and effort. It means helping others become better people. It demands our time, money, and personal involvement. No individual has the capacity to express love to a whole community,

but the body of Christ in your town does. Look for people who need your love, and look for ways you and your fellow believers can love your community for Christ.

● **12:10** We can honor others in one of two ways. One involves ulterior motives. We honor our bosses so they will reward us, our employees so they will work harder, the wealthy so they will contribute to our cause, the powerful so they will use their power for us and not against us. God's way involves love. As Christians, we honor people because they have been created in God's image, because they are our brothers and sisters in Christ, and because they have a unique contribution to make to Christ's church. Does God's way of honoring others sound too difficult for your competitive nature? Why not try to outdo one another in showing honor? Put others first!

● **12:13** Christian hospitality differs from social entertaining. Entertaining focuses on the host: The home must be spotless; the food must be well prepared and abundant; the host must appear relaxed and good-natured. Hospitality, by contrast, focuses on the guests' needs, such as a place to stay, nourishing food, a listening ear, or just acceptance. Hospitality can happen in a messy home. It can happen around a dinner table where the main dish is canned soup. It can even happen while the host and the guest are doing chores together. Don't hesitate to offer hospitality just because you are too tired, too busy, or not wealthy enough to entertain.

12:16 Many people use their contacts and relationships for selfish ambition. They select those people who will help them climb the social ladder. Christ demonstrated and taught that we should treat all people with respect—those of a different race, the handicapped, the poor, young and old, male and female. We must never consider others as being beneath us. Paul says we need to live in harmony with others and not be too proud to enjoy the company of ordinary people. Are you able to do humble tasks with others? Do you welcome conversation with unattractive, non-prestigious people? Are you willing to befriend newcomers and entry-level people? Or do you relate only to those who will help you get ahead?

[17]Never pay back evil with more evil. Do things in such a way that everyone can see you are honorable. [18]Do all that you can to live in peace with everyone.

[19]Dear friends, never take revenge. Leave that to the righteous anger of God. For the Scriptures say,

> "I will take revenge;
> I will pay them back,"*
> says the LORD.

[20]Instead,

> "If your enemies are hungry, feed them.
> If they are thirsty, give them something to drink.
> In doing this, you will heap
> burning coals of shame on their heads."*

[21]Don't let evil conquer you, but conquer evil by doing good.

Respect for Authority

13 Everyone must submit to governing authorities. For all authority comes from God, and those in positions of authority have been placed there by God. [2]So anyone who rebels against authority is rebelling against what God has instituted, and they will be punished. [3]For the authorities do not strike fear in people who are doing right, but in those who are doing wrong. Would you like to live without fear of the authorities? Do what is right, and they will honor you. [4]The authorities are God's servants, sent for your good. But if you are doing wrong, of course you should be afraid, for they have the power to punish you. They are God's servants, sent for the very purpose of punishing those who do what is wrong. [5]So you must submit to them, not only to avoid punishment, but also to keep a clear conscience.

[6]Pay your taxes, too, for these same reasons. For government workers need to be paid. They are serving God in what they do. [7]Give to everyone what you owe them: Pay your taxes and government fees to those who collect them, and give respect and honor to those who are in authority.

12:19 Deut 32:35. **12:20** Prov 25:21-22.

Margin references:
12:17 Prov 3:4; 20:22 / 1 Thes 5:15
12:19 †Deut 32:35
12:20 †Prov 25:21-22 / Matt 5:44
13:1 Dan 2:21 / John 19:11 / Titus 3:1
13:3 1 Pet 2:13-14
13:5 1 Pet 2:13
13:7 Matt 22:21 / Mark 12:17 / Luke 20:25

• **12:17-21** These verses summarize the core of Christian living. If we love someone the way Christ loves us, we will be willing to forgive. If we have experienced God's grace, we will want to pass it on to others. And remember, grace is *undeserved* favor. By giving an enemy a drink, we're not excusing his misdeeds. We're recognizing him, forgiving him, and loving him in spite of his sins—just as Christ did for us.

• **12:19-21** In this day of lawsuits and incessant demands for legal rights, Paul's command sounds almost impossible. When someone hurts you deeply, instead of giving him what he deserves, Paul says to befriend him. Why does Paul tell us to forgive our enemies? (1) Forgiveness may break a cycle of retaliation and lead to mutual reconciliation. (2) It may make the enemy feel ashamed and change his or her ways. (3) By contrast, repaying evil for evil hurts you just as much as it hurts your enemy. Even if your enemy never repents, forgiving him or her will free you of a heavy load of bitterness.

• **12:19-21** Forgiveness involves both attitudes and actions. If you find it difficult to *feel* forgiving toward someone who has hurt you, try responding with kind actions. If appropriate, tell this person that you would like to heal your relationship. Lend a helping hand. Send him or her a gift. Smile at him or her. Many times you will discover that right actions lead to right feelings.

• **13:1** Are there times when we should not obey the government? We should never allow government to force us to disobey God. Jesus and his apostles never disobeyed the government for personal reasons; when they disobeyed, it was in order to follow God's moral standards. Their disobedience was not cheap: They were threatened, beaten, thrown into jail, tortured, or executed for their convictions. Like them, if we are compelled to disobey, we must be ready to accept the consequences.

• **13:1ff** Christians understand Romans 13 in different ways. All Christians agree that we are to live at peace with the state as long as the state allows us to live by our religious convictions. For hundreds of years, however, there have been at least three interpretations of how we are to do this:

(1) Some Christians believe that the state is so corrupt that Christians should have as little to do with it as possible. Although they should be good citizens as long as they can do so without compromising their beliefs, they should not work for the government, vote in elections, or serve in the military.

(2) Others believe that God has given the state authority in certain areas and the church authority in others. Christians can be loyal to both and can work for either. They should not, however, confuse the two. In this view, church and state are concerned with two totally different spheres—the spiritual and the physical—and thus complement each other but do not work together.

(3) Still others believe that Christians have a responsibility to make the state better. They can do this politically, by electing Christian or other high-principled leaders. They can also do this morally, by serving as an influence for good in society. In this view, church and state ideally work together for the good of all.

None of these views advocate rebelling against or refusing to obey the government's laws or regulations unless those laws clearly require you to violate the moral standards revealed by God. Wherever we find ourselves, we must be responsible citizens, as well as responsible Christians.

• **13:3, 4** Willingly or unwittingly, people in authority are God's servants. They are allowed their positions in order to do good. When authorities are unjust, however, upright people are afraid. When authorities are just, people who are doing right have nothing to fear. This provides our principal motivation to pray for our leaders. Praying for those in authority over us will also mean that we will watch them closely. If we pray diligently for our leaders, we will be functioning as God's sentinels.

Love Fulfills God's Requirements

13:8
Matt 5:34
John 13:34

13:9
Exod 20:13-15, 17
†Lev 19:18
†Deut 5:17-19, 21

13:11
1 Cor 7:29-31
1 Thes 5:5-6
Jas 5:8
1 Pet 4:7

13:12
Eph 5:11; 6:13
1 Thes 5:8

13:13
Luke 21:34
Eph 5:18

8Owe nothing to anyone—except for your obligation to love one another. If you love your neighbor, you will fulfill the requirements of God's law. 9For the commandments say, "You must not commit adultery. You must not murder. You must not steal. You must not covet."* These—and other such commandments—are summed up in this one commandment: "Love your neighbor as yourself."* 10Love does no wrong to others, so love fulfills the requirements of God's law.

11This is all the more urgent, for you know how late it is; time is running out. Wake up, for our salvation is nearer now than when we first believed. 12The night is almost gone; the day of salvation will soon be here. So remove your dark deeds like dirty clothes, and put on the shining armor of right living. 13Because we belong to the day, we must live decent lives for all to see. Don't participate in the darkness of wild parties and drunkenness, or in sexual promiscuity and immoral living, or in quarreling and jealousy. 14Instead, clothe yourself with the presence of the Lord Jesus Christ. And don't let yourself think about ways to indulge your evil desires.

The Danger of Criticism

14:1
1 Cor 9:22

14:2
1 Cor 10:25-27

14 Accept other believers who are weak in faith, and don't argue with them about what they think is right or wrong. 2For instance, one person believes it's all right to eat

13:9a Exod 20:13-15, 17.   **13:9b** Lev 19:18.

• **13:8** Why is love for others called an obligation? We are permanently in debt to Christ for the lavish love he has poured out on us. The only way we can even begin to repay this debt is by fulfilling our obligation to love others in turn. Because Christ's love will always be infinitely greater than ours, we will always have the obligation to love our neighbors.

• **13:9** Somehow many of us have gotten the idea that self-love is wrong. But if this were the case, it would be pointless to love our neighbors as ourselves. But Paul explains what he means by self-love. Even if you have low self-esteem, you probably don't willingly let yourself go hungry. You take care of your body and may even exercise. You clothe yourself reasonably well. You make sure there's a roof over your head. You try not to let yourself be cheated or injured. This is the kind of love we need to have for our neighbors. Do we see that others are fed, clothed, and housed as well as they can be? Are we concerned about issues of social justice? Loving others as ourselves means actively working to see that their needs are met. Interestingly, people who focus on others rather than on themselves rarely suffer from low self-esteem.

• **13:10** Christians must obey the law of love, which supersedes both religious and civil laws. How easy it is to excuse our indifference to others merely because we have no legal obligation to help them and even to justify harming them if our actions are technically legal! But Jesus does not leave loopholes in the law of love. Whenever love demands it, we are to go beyond human legal requirements and imitate the God of love. See James 2:8, 9; 4:11 and 1 Peter 2:16, 17 for more about this law of love.

• **13:12-14** The "night" refers to the present evil time. The "day" refers to the time of Christ's return. Some people are surprised that Paul lists fighting and jealousy with the gross and obvious sins of drunkenness and immorality. Like Jesus in his Sermon on the Mount (Matthew 5–7), Paul considers attitudes as important as actions. Just as hatred leads to murder, so jealousy leads to strife and lust to adultery. When Christ returns, he wants to find his people clean on the inside as well as on the outside.

• **13:14** How do we clothe ourselves with the presence of the Lord Jesus Christ? First, we identify with Christ by being baptized (Galatians 3:27). This shows our solidarity with other Christians and with the death, burial, and resurrection of Jesus Christ. Second, we exemplify the qualities Jesus showed while he was here on earth (love, humility, truth, service). In a sense, we role-play what Jesus would do in our situation (see Ephesians 4:24-32; Colossians 3:10-17). We also must avoid those situations that open the door to gratifying sinful desires.

• **14:1** Who is weak in faith and who is strong? We are all weak

in some areas and strong in others. Our faith is strong in an area if we can survive contact with worldly people without falling into their patterns. It is weak in an area if we must avoid certain activities, people, or places in order to protect our spiritual life. It is important to take self-inventory in order to find out our strengths and weaknesses. Whenever in doubt, we should ask, Can I do that without sinning? Can I influence others for good, rather than being influenced by them?

In areas of strength, we should not fear being defiled by the world; rather we should go and serve God. In areas of weakness, we need to be cautious. If we have a strong faith but shelter it, we are not doing Christ's work in the world. If we have a weak faith but expose it, we are being extremely foolish.

• **14:1** This verse assumes there will be differences of opinion in the church about what is right or wrong. Paul says we are not to quarrel about issues that are matters of opinion. Differences should not be feared or avoided but accepted and handled with love. Don't expect everyone, even in the best possible church, to agree on every subject. Through sharing ideas we can come to a fuller understanding of what the Bible teaches. Accept, listen to, and respect others. Differences of opinion need not cause division. They can be a source of learning and richness in our relationships.

• **14:1ff** What is weak faith? Paul is speaking about immature faith that has not yet developed the muscle it needs to stand against external pressures. For example, if a person who once worshiped idols became a Christian, he might understand perfectly well that Christ saved him through faith and that idols have no real power. Still, because of his past associations, he might be badly shaken if he unknowingly ate meat that had been used in idol worship. If a person who once worshiped God on the required Jewish holy days became a Christian, he might well know that Christ saved him through faith, not through his keeping of the law. Still, when the festival days came, he might feel empty and unfaithful if he didn't dedicate those days to God.

Paul responds to both weak brothers in love. Both are acting according to their consciences, but their honest convictions do not need to be made into rules for the church. Certainly some issues are central to the faith and worth fighting for, but many are based on individual differences and should not be legislated. Our principle should be: In essentials, unity; in nonessentials, liberty; in everything, love.

• **14:2** Eating "anything" may refer to a strong Christian being free from dietary restrictions, or it may refer to his eating meat offered to idols. The person weaker in the faith, however, may eat only vegetables and refuse to eat meat that has been offered to

anything. But another believer with a sensitive conscience will eat only vegetables. ³Those who feel free to eat anything must not look down on those who don't. And those who don't eat certain foods must not condemn those who do, for God has accepted them. ⁴Who are you to condemn someone else's servants? Their own master will judge whether they stand or fall. And with the Lord's help, they will stand and receive his approval.

⁵In the same way, some think one day is more holy than another day, while others think every day is alike. You should each be fully convinced that whichever day you choose is acceptable. ⁶Those who worship the Lord on a special day do it to honor him. Those who eat any kind of food do so to honor the Lord, since they give thanks to God before eating. And those who refuse to eat certain foods also want to please the Lord and give thanks to God. ⁷For we don't live for ourselves or die for ourselves. ⁸If we live, it's to honor the Lord. And if we die, it's to honor the Lord. So whether we live or die, we belong to the Lord. ⁹Christ died and rose again for this very purpose—to be Lord both of the living and of the dead.

¹⁰So why do you condemn another believer*? Why do you look down on another believer? Remember, we will all stand before the judgment seat of God. ¹¹For the Scriptures say,

"'As surely as I live,' says the LORD,
'every knee will bend to me,
    and every tongue will confess and give praise to God.*'"

¹²Yes, each of us will give a personal account to God. ¹³So let's stop condemning each other. Decide instead to live in such a way that you will not cause another believer to stumble and fall.

¹⁴I know and am convinced on the authority of the Lord Jesus that no food, in and of itself, is wrong to eat. But if someone believes it is wrong, then for that person it is wrong. ¹⁵And if another believer is distressed by what you eat, you are not acting in love if you eat it. Don't let your eating ruin someone for whom Christ died. ¹⁶Then you will not be criticized for doing something you believe is good. ¹⁷For the Kingdom of God is not a matter of what we eat or drink, but of living a life of goodness and peace and joy in the Holy Spirit. ¹⁸If you serve Christ with this attitude, you will please God, and others will approve of you, too. ¹⁹So then, let us aim for harmony in the church and try to build each other up.

14:10 Greek *your brother;* also in 14:10b, 13, 15, 21.   14:11 Or *confess allegiance to God.* Isa 49:18; 45:23 (Greek version).

14:3
Col 2:16

14:4
Matt 7:1

14:5
Gal 4:10

14:6
1 Cor 10:30

14:7
2 Cor 5:15
Gal 2:20

14:8
Phil 1:20
1 Thes 5:10

14:9
Rev 1:18

14:10
Matt 25:31-32
Acts 17:31
2 Cor 5:10

14:11
†Isa 45:23; 49:18

14:12
Gal 6:5

14:13
Matt 7:1
2 Cor 6:3

14:14
Acts 10:15
1 Cor 8:7

14:15
1 Cor 8:11-13

14:16
1 Cor 10:30
Titus 2:5

14:17
Rom 15:13
Gal 5:22

14:19
Rom 12:18; 15:2

---

idols. But how would Christians end up eating meat that had been offered to idols? The ancient system of sacrifice was at the center of the religious, social, and domestic life of the Roman world. After a sacrifice was presented to a god in a pagan temple, only part of it was burned. The remainder was often sent to the market to be sold. Thus, a Christian might easily—even unknowingly—buy such meat in the marketplace or eat it at the home of a friend. Should a Christian question the source of his meat? Some thought there was nothing wrong with eating meat that had been offered to idols because idols were worthless. Others carefully checked the source of their meat or gave up meat altogether, in order to avoid a guilty conscience. The problem was especially acute for Christians who had once been idol worshipers. For them, such a strong reminder of their pagan days might weaken their newfound faith. Paul also deals with this problem in 1 Corinthians 8.

• **14:10-12** Each person is accountable to Christ, not to others. While the church must be uncompromising in its stand against activities that are expressly forbidden by Scripture (adultery, homosexuality, murder, theft), it should not create additional rules and regulations and give them equal standing with God's law. Many times Christians base their moral judgments on opinion, personal dislikes, or cultural bias rather than on the Word of God. When they do this, they show that their own faith is weak; they do not think that God is powerful enough to guide his children. When we stand before God and give a personal account of our life, we won't be worried about what our Christian neighbor has done (see 2 Corinthians 5:10).

• **14:13** Both strong and weak Christians can cause their brothers and sisters to stumble. The strong but insensitive Christian may flaunt his or her freedom and intentionally offend others' consciences. The scrupulous but weak Christian may try to fence others in with petty rules and regulations, thus causing dissension. Paul wants his readers to be both strong in the faith and sensitive to others' needs. Because we are all strong in some areas and weak in others, we need to constantly monitor the effects of our behavior on others.

• **14:13ff** Some Christians use an invisible weaker brother to support their own opinions, prejudices, or standards. "You must live by these standards," they say, "or you will be offending the weaker brother." In truth, the person would often be offending no one but the speaker. While Paul urges us to be sensitive to those whose faith may be harmed by our actions, we should not sacrifice our liberty in Christ just to satisfy the selfish motives of those who are trying to force their opinions on us. Neither fear them nor criticize them, but follow Christ as closely as you can.

14:14 At the Jerusalem council (Acts 15), the Jewish church in Jerusalem asked the Gentile church in Antioch not to eat meat that had been sacrificed to idols. Paul was at the Jerusalem council, and he accepted this request, not because he felt that eating such meat was wrong in itself, but because this practice would deeply offend many Jewish believers. Paul did not think the issue was worth dividing the church over; his desire was to promote unity. So he concludes, "if someone believes it is wrong, then for that person it is wrong." Paul's practice was to honor, as far as possible, the convictions of others.

Believers are called to accept one another without judging our varied opinions. However, when the situation has to be faced, how should we deal with those who disagree with us? Paul's response is that all believers should act in love so as to maintain peace in the church.

14:20
Acts 10:15
1 Cor 8:9-12
14:21
1 Cor 8:13
14:22
1 Jn 3:21

²⁰Don't tear apart the work of God over what you eat. Remember, all foods are acceptable, but it is wrong to eat something if it makes another person stumble. ²¹It is better not to eat meat or drink wine or do anything else if it might cause another believer to stumble. ²²You may believe there's nothing wrong with what you are doing, but keep it between yourself and God. Blessed are those who don't feel guilty for doing something they have decided is right. ²³But if you have doubts about whether or not you should eat something, you are sinning if you go ahead and do it. For you are not following your convictions. If you do anything you believe is not right, you are sinning.

Living to Please Others

15:2
Rom 14:19
1 Cor 9:19; 10:24
Gal 6:2
15:3
†Ps 69:9
15:4
Rom 4:23-24
2 Tim 3:16
15:5
1 Cor 1:10
2 Cor 1:3
15:6
Rev 1:6
15:7
Rom 14:1
15:8
Matt 15:24
Acts 3:25-26
2 Cor 1:20
15:9
†2 Sam 22:50
†Ps 18:49
15:10
†Deut 32:43

15:11
†Ps 117:1

15:12
†Isa 11:10
Rev 5:5; 22:16

15 We who are strong must be considerate of those who are sensitive about things like this. We must not just please ourselves. ²We should help others do what is right and build them up in the Lord. ³For even Christ didn't live to please himself. As the Scriptures say, "The insults of those who insult you, O God, have fallen on me."* ⁴Such things were written in the Scriptures long ago to teach us. And the Scriptures give us hope and encouragement as we wait patiently for God's promises to be fulfilled.

⁵May God, who gives this patience and encouragement, help you live in complete harmony with each other, as is fitting for followers of Christ Jesus. ⁶Then all of you can join together with one voice, giving praise and glory to God, the Father of our Lord Jesus Christ.

⁷Therefore, accept each other just as Christ has accepted you so that God will be given glory. ⁸Remember that Christ came as a servant to the Jews* to show that God is true to the promises he made to their ancestors. ⁹He also came so that the Gentiles might give glory to God for his mercies to them. That is what the psalmist meant when he wrote:

"For this, I will praise you among the Gentiles;
   I will sing praises to your name."*

¹⁰And in another place it is written,

"Rejoice with his people,
   you Gentiles."*

¹¹And yet again,

"Praise the Lᴏʀᴅ, all you Gentiles.
   Praise him, all you people of the earth."*

¹²And in another place Isaiah said,

"The heir to David's throne* will come,
   and he will rule over the Gentiles.
They will place their hope on him."*

¹³I pray that God, the source of hope, will fill you completely with joy and peace because you trust in him. Then you will overflow with confident hope through the power of the Holy Spirit.

15:3 Greek *who insult you have fallen on me.* Ps 69:9.   **15:8** Greek *servant of circumcision.*   **15:9** Ps 18:49.
15:10 Deut 32:43.   **15:11** Ps 117:1.   **15:12a** Greek *The root of Jesse.* David was the son of Jesse.
15:12b Isa 11:10 (Greek version).

• **14:20, 21** Sin is not just a private matter. Everything we do affects others, and we have to think of them constantly. God created us to be interdependent, not independent. We who are strong in our faith must, without pride or condescension, treat others with love, patience, and self-restraint.

• **14:23** We try to steer clear of actions forbidden by Scripture, of course, but sometimes Scripture is silent. Then we should follow our consciences. "If you do anything you believe is not right, you are sinning" means that to go against a conviction will leave a person with a guilty or uneasy conscience. When God shows us that something is wrong for us, we should avoid it. But we should not look down on other Christians who exercise their freedom in those areas.

15:4 The knowledge of the Scriptures affects our attitude toward the present and the future. The more we know about what God has done in years past, the greater the confidence we have about

what he will do in the days ahead. We need to diligently read our Bibles so we may have confidence that God's will is best for us.

15:5-7 The Roman church was a diverse community. It was made up of Jews and Gentiles, slaves and free people, rich and poor, strong and weak. So it was difficult for them to accept one another. Accepting means taking people into our homes as well as into our hearts, sharing meals and activities, and avoiding racial and economic discrimination. We must go out of our way to avoid favoritism. Consciously spend time greeting those you don't normally talk to, minimize differences, and seek common ground for fellowship. In this way you are accepting others as Christ has accepted you, and God is given glory.

2. Personal notes

Paul's Reason for Writing

[14]I am fully convinced, my dear brothers and sisters,* that you are full of goodness. You know these things so well you can teach each other all about them. [15]Even so, I have been bold enough to write about some of these points, knowing that all you need is this reminder. For by God's grace, [16]I am a special messenger from Christ Jesus to you Gentiles. I bring you the Good News so that I might present you as an acceptable offering to God, made holy by the Holy Spirit. [17]So I have reason to be enthusiastic about all Christ Jesus has done through me in my service to God. [18]Yet I dare not boast about anything except what Christ has done through me, bringing the Gentiles to God by my message and by the way I worked among them. [19]They were convinced by the power of miraculous signs and wonders and by the power of God's Spirit.* In this way, I have fully presented the Good News of Christ from Jerusalem all the way to Illyricum.*

[20]My ambition has always been to preach the Good News where the name of Christ has never been heard, rather than where a church has already been started by someone else. [21]I have been following the plan spoken of in the Scriptures, where it says,

"Those who have never been told about him will see,
  and those who have never heard of him will understand."*

[22]In fact, my visit to you has been delayed so long because I have been preaching in these places.

Paul's Travel Plans

[23]But now I have finished my work in these regions, and after all these long years of waiting, I am eager to visit you. [24]I am planning to go to Spain, and when I do, I will stop off in Rome. And after I have enjoyed your fellowship for a little while, you can provide for my journey.

[25]But before I come, I must go to Jerusalem to take a gift to the believers* there. [26]For you see, the believers in Macedonia and Achaia* have eagerly taken up an offering for the poor among the believers in Jerusalem. [27]They were glad to do this because they feel they owe a real debt to them. Since the Gentiles received the spiritual blessings of the Good News from the believers in Jerusalem, they feel the least they can do in return is to help them financially. [28]As soon as I have delivered this money and completed this good deed of theirs, I will come to see you on my way to Spain. [29]And I am sure that when I come, Christ will richly bless our time together.

[30]Dear brothers and sisters, I urge you in the name of our Lord Jesus Christ to join in my struggle by praying to God for me. Do this because of your love for me, given to you by the Holy Spirit. [31]Pray that I will be rescued from those in Judea who refuse to obey God. Pray

15:14
2 Pet 1:12
15:15
Rom 1:5; 12:3
15:16
Phil 2:17
15:17
Phil 3:3
15:18
Rom 1:5
15:19
Acts 19:11
1 Cor 2:4
1 Thes 1:5
15:20
Rom 1:15
1 Cor 3:10
2 Cor 10:13, 15
15:21
†Isa 52:15
15:22
Rom 1:10-13
1 Thes 2:18
15:23
Acts 19:21
Rom 1:10-11
15:24
1 Cor 16:6
15:25
Acts 19:21; 20:22
15:26
1 Cor 16:1
2 Cor 8:1; 9:2
15:27
1 Cor 9:11
15:29
Rom 1:10-11
15:30
2 Cor 1:11
Col 1:8; 4:12
15:31
2 Thes 3:2

15:14 Greek *brothers;* also in 15:30.   **15:19a** Other manuscripts read *the Spirit;* still others read *the Holy Spirit.*
15:19b *Illyricum* was a region northeast of Italy.   **15:21** Isa 52:15 (Greek version).   **15:25** Greek *God's holy people;*
also in 15:26, 31.   **15:26** *Macedonia* and *Achaia* were the northern and southern regions of Greece.

15:19 Illyricum was a Roman territory on the Adriatic Sea between present-day Italy and Greece. It covered much the same territory as present-day Yugoslavia. See the map on p. 5.

15:20 Paul says that he has "ambition." Ambition can be a difficult topic for Christians because we see so many bad examples of ambitious people who claw their way to the top. But certainly that isn't the kind of ambition one sees in Paul. Instead of looking out for himself and working hard for personal advancement, he was ambitious to serve God—for Paul that meant to "preach the Good News where the name of Christ has never been heard." Are you ambitious for God? Do you want, more than anything else, to please him and to do his will? Ask God for "holy ambition."

• **15:22** Paul wanted to visit the church at Rome, but he had delayed his visit because he had heard many good reports about the believers there and knew they were doing well on their own. It was more important for him to preach in areas that had not yet heard the Good News.

• **15:23, 24** Paul was referring to the completion of his work in Corinth, the city from which he most likely wrote this letter. Most of Paul's three-month stay in Achaia (see Acts 20:3) was probably spent in Corinth. He believed that he had accomplished

what God wanted him to do there, and he was looking forward to taking the Good News to new lands west of Rome. When Paul eventually went to Rome, however, it was as a prisoner (see Acts 28). Tradition says that Paul was released for a time and that he used this opportunity to go to Spain to preach the Good News. This journey is not mentioned in the book of Acts.

15:28 Paul's future plan was to go to Spain because Spain was at the very western end of the civilized world. He wanted to bring Christianity there. Also, Spain had many great minds and influential leaders in the Roman world (Lucan, Martial, Hadrian), and perhaps Paul thought Christianity would advance greatly in such an atmosphere.

• **15:30** Too often we see prayer as a time for comfort, reflection, or making requests to God. But here Paul urges believers to join in his *struggle* by means of prayer. Prayer is a weapon that all believers should use in interceding for others. Many of us know believers who are living in difficult places in order to communicate the gospel. Sending them funds is part of joining them in their struggles, but prayer is also a crucial way of being with them. Missionaries strongly desire the prayers of those who have sent them out. Do your prayers reflect that struggle on their behalf?

15:32
Phlm 1:7

15:33
Rom 16:20
Heb 13:20

also that the believers there will be willing to accept the donation* I am taking to Jerusalem. 32 Then, by the will of God, I will be able to come to you with a joyful heart, and we will be an encouragement to each other.

33 And now may God, who gives us his peace, be with you all. Amen.*

Paul Greets His Friends

16:1
Acts 18:18

16:2
Phil 2:29

16 I commend to you our sister Phoebe, who is a deacon in the church in Cenchrea. 2 Welcome her in the Lord as one who is worthy of honor among God's people. Help her in whatever she needs, for she has been helpful to many, and especially to me.

3 Give my greetings to Priscilla and Aquila, my co-workers in the ministry of Christ Jesus. 4 In fact, they once risked their lives for me. I am thankful to them, and so are all the Gentile churches. 5 Also give my greetings to the church that meets in their home.

16:5
1 Cor 16:15, 19
Col 4:15
Phlm 1:2

16:7
Rom 16:11, 21
Col 4:10
Phlm 1:23

Greet my dear friend Epenetus. He was the first person from the province of Asia to become a follower of Christ. 6 Give my greetings to Mary, who has worked so hard for your benefit. 7 Greet Andronicus and Junia,* my fellow Jews,* who were in prison with me. They are highly respected among the apostles and became followers of Christ before I did. 8 Greet Ampliatus, my dear friend in the Lord. 9 Greet Urbanus, our co-worker in Christ, and my dear friend Stachys.

16:10
Acts 11:14

16:11
Rom 16:7, 21

16:13
Mark 15:21
2 Jn 1:1

10 Greet Apelles, a good man whom Christ approves. And give my greetings to the believers from the household of Aristobulus. 11 Greet Herodion, my fellow Jew.* Greet the Lord's people from the household of Narcissus. 12 Give my greetings to Tryphena and Tryphosa, the Lord's workers, and to dear Persis, who has worked so hard for the Lord. 13 Greet Rufus, whom the Lord picked out to be his very own; and also his dear mother, who has been a mother to me.

16:16
1 Cor 16:20
1 Thes 5:26
1 Pet 5:14

14 Give my greetings to Asyncritus, Phlegon, Hermes, Patrobas, Hermas, and the brothers and sisters* who meet with them. 15 Give my greetings to Philologus, Julia, Nereus and his sister, and to Olympas and all the believers* who meet with them. 16 Greet each other in Christian love.* All the churches of Christ send you their greetings.

Paul's Final Instructions

16:17
1 Cor 5:9, 11
2 Thes 3:6
2 Tim 3:5
Titus 3:10
2 Jn 1:10

16:18
Phil 3:19
Col 2:4
2 Pet 2:3

16:19
Matt 10:16

17 And now I make one more appeal, my dear brothers and sisters. Watch out for people who cause divisions and upset people's faith by teaching things contrary to what you have been taught. Stay away from them. 18 Such people are not serving Christ our Lord; they are serving their own personal interests. By smooth talk and glowing words they deceive innocent people. 19 But everyone knows that you are obedient to the Lord. This makes me very happy. I

15:31 Greek *the ministry;* other manuscripts read *the gift.* **15:33** Some manuscripts do not include *Amen.* One very early manuscript places 16:25-27 here. **16:7a** *Junia* is a feminine name. Some late manuscripts accent the word so it reads *Junias,* a masculine name; still others read *Julia* (feminine). **16:7b** Or *compatriots;* also in 16:21. **16:11** Or *compatriot.* **16:14** Greek *brothers;* also in 16:17. **16:15** Greek *all of God's holy people.* **16:16** Greek *with a sacred kiss.*

15:33 This phrase sounds like it should signal the end of the letter, and it does pronounce the end of Paul's teaching. He concludes his letter, then, with personal greetings and remarks.

• **16:1, 2** Phoebe was known as a "deacon," or servant and helper. Apparently she was a wealthy person who helped support Paul's ministry. Phoebe was highly regarded in the church, and she may have delivered this letter from Corinth to Rome. This provides evidence that women had important roles in the early church. Cenchrea, the town where Phoebe lived, was the eastern port of Corinth, six miles from the city center.

• **16:3** Priscilla and Aquila were a married couple who had become Paul's close friends. They, along with all other Jews, had been expelled from Rome by the emperor (Acts 18:2, 3) and had moved to Corinth. There they met Paul and invited him to live with them. They were Christians before they met Paul and probably told him much about the Roman church. Like Paul, Priscilla and Aquila were missionaries. They helped believers in Ephesus (Acts 18:18-28), in Rome when they were allowed to return, and again at Ephesus (2 Timothy 4:19).

16:3 Priscilla and Aquila ministered effectively behind the scenes. Their tools were hospitality, friendship, and person-to-person teaching. They were not public speakers, but private evangelists. For some of the Romans, their home was used for church meetings (16:5). Priscilla and Aquila challenge us with what a

couple can do together to serve Christ. Do we regard our families and homes as gifts through which God can accomplish his work? How might God want to use your home and family to serve him?

• **16:5ff** Paul's personal greetings went to Romans and Greeks, Jews and Gentiles, men and women, prisoners and prominent citizens. The church's base was broad, crossing cultural, social, and economic lines. From this list we learn that the Christian community was mobile. Though Paul had not yet been to Rome, he had met these people in other places on his journeys.

• **16:7** The fact that Andronicus and Junia were "highly respected among the apostles" could mean they had distinguished themselves as apostles. They may have been a husband and wife team. Paul notes that they were "fellow Jews" who at one time had been in prison with him.

• **16:17-20** When we read books or listen to sermons, we should check the content of what is written or said so that we won't be fooled by smooth talk and glowing words. Christians who study God's Word, asking him to reveal the truth, will not be fooled, even though superficial Christians may easily be taken in. For an example of believers who carefully checked God's Word, see Acts 17:10-12.

want you to be wise in doing right and to stay innocent of any wrong. 20The God of peace will soon crush Satan under your feet. May the grace of our Lord Jesus* be with you.

21Timothy, my fellow worker, sends you his greetings, as do Lucius, Jason, and Sosipater, my fellow Jews.

22I, Tertius, the one writing this letter for Paul, send my greetings, too, as one of the Lord's followers.

23Gaius says hello to you. He is my host and also serves as host to the whole church. Erastus, the city treasurer, sends you his greetings, and so does our brother Quartus.*

25Now all glory to God, who is able to make you strong, just as my Good News says. This message about Jesus Christ has revealed his plan for you Gentiles, a plan kept secret from the beginning of time. 26But now as the prophets* foretold and as the eternal God has commanded, this message is made known to all Gentiles everywhere, so that they too might believe and obey him. 27All glory to the only wise God, through Jesus Christ, forever. Amen.

16:20 Gen 3:15

16:21 Acts 13:1; 16:1; 17:5

16:25 1 Cor 2:1
Eph 1:9; 3:3-5
Col 1:26-27; 2:2
2 Tim 1:9-10
1 Pet 1:20

16:26 Rom 1:2, 5

16:27 Rom 11:36

16:20 Some manuscripts read *Lord Jesus Christ.*   **16:23** Some manuscripts add verse 24, *May the grace of our Lord Jesus Christ be with you all. Amen.* Still others add this sentence after verse 27.   **16:26** Greek *the prophetic writings.*

- **16:21** Timothy was a key person in the growth of the early church, traveling with Paul on his second missionary journey (Acts 16:1-3). Later Paul wrote two letters to him as he worked to strengthen the churches in Ephesus—1 and 2 Timothy. See his Profile in the book of 1 Timothy 2, p. 2059.

16:25-27 Paul exclaims that it is wonderful to be alive when the plan, God's secret—his way of saving the Gentiles—is becoming known throughout the world! All the Old Testament prophecies were coming true, and God was using Paul as his instrument to tell this Good News.

- **16:25-27** As Jerusalem was the center of Jewish life, Rome was the world's political, religious, social, and economic center.

There the major governmental decisions were made, and from there the Good News spread to the ends of the earth. The church in Rome was a cosmopolitan mixture of Jews, Gentiles, slaves, free people, men, women, Roman citizens, and world travelers; therefore, it had potential for both great influence and great conflict.

Paul had not yet been to Rome to meet all the Christians there, and, of course, he has not yet met us. We, too, live in a cosmopolitan setting with the entire world open to us. We also have the potential for both widespread influence and wrenching conflict. Listen carefully to Paul's teachings about unity, service, and love so you may apply them.

STUDY QUESTIONS

Thirteen lessons for individual or group study

It's always exciting to get more than you expect. And that's what you'll find in this Bible study guide—much more than you expect. Our goal was to write thoughtful, practical, dependable, and application-oriented studies of God's word.

This study guide contains the complete text of the selected Bible book. The commentary is accurate, complete, and loaded with unique charts, maps, and profiles of Bible people.

With the Bible text, extensive notes and helps, and questions to guide discussion, Life Application Bible Studies have everything you need in one place.

The lessons in this Bible study guide will work for large classes as well as small-group studies. To get everyone involved in your discussions, encourage participants to answer the questions before each meeting.

Each lesson is divided into five easy-to-lead sections. The section called "Reflect" introduces you and the members of your group to a specific area of life touched by the lesson. "Read" shows which chapters to read and which notes and other features to use. Additional questions help you understand the passage. "Realize" brings into focus the biblical principle to be learned with questions, a special insight, or both. "Respond" helps you make connections with your own situation and personal needs. The questions are designed to help you find areas in your life where you can apply the biblical truths. "Resolve" helps you map out action plans for that day.

Begin and end each lesson with prayer, asking for the Holy Spirit's guidance, direction, and wisdom.

Recommended time allotments for each section of a lesson are as follows:

Segment	60 minutes	90 minutes
Reflect on your life	*5 minutes*	*10 minutes*
Read the passage	*10 minutes*	*15 minutes*
Realize the principle	*15 minutes*	*20 minutes*
Respond to the message	*20 minutes*	*30 minutes*
Resolve to take action	*10 minutes*	*15 minutes*

All five sections work together to help a person learn the lessons, live out the principles, and obey the commands taught in the Bible.

Also, at the end of each lesson, there is a section entitled "More for studying other themes in this section." These questions will help you lead the group in studying other parts of each section not covered in depth by the main lesson.

But don't just listen to God's word. You must do what it says. Otherwise, you are only fooling yourselves. For if you listen to the word and don't obey, it is like glancing at your face in a mirror. You see yourself, walk away, and forget what you look like. But if you look carefully into the perfect law that sets you free, and if you do what it says and don't forget what you heard, then God will bless you for doing it (James 1:22-25).

LESSON 1
THE GOSPEL AT THE CROSSROADS
ROMANS 1:1-17

R
REFLECT
on your life

1 Choose a sport and describe what is meant by the fundamentals. What are the fundamentals of faith in Christ?

_____

_____

_____

_____

R
READ
the passage

Read the two pages of introductory material on Romans, Romans 1:1-17, and the following notes:

❏ 1:1 ❏ 1:3-5 ❏ 1:5 ❏ 1:6, 7 ❏ 1:7 ❏ 1:8 ❏ 1:9, 10

❏ 1:11-13 ❏ 1:14

2 These opening verses tell us some important facts about the messenger, the message, and the audience of this letter. Summarize what you know about each.

Messenger	Message	Audience
_____	_____	_____
_____	_____	_____
_____	_____	_____

3 Paul's understanding of the gospel is rooted in Old Testament prophecy, Jewish history, and personal experience. What key events in his life formed the foundation of his faith?

_____

_____

_____

_____

4 Why was Paul ideally suited to address this particular body of believers, even though he had never visited them?

_____

_____

_____

_____

5 Why was the church in Rome such an important group of believers to influence?

_____

_____

_____

6 Why was Paul thankful for the church in Rome?

_____

_____

_____

REALIZE
the principle

7 What did Paul want to give the believers in Rome? How might his visit encourage them? If Paul visited your church, how might he be encouraged?

_____

_____

_____

_____

_____

_____

"Believe and obey" summarizes the structure of Romans. The first part of the letter addresses the issue of faith, and the final chapters deal with how we must live out our faith in everyday life. The Christian faith is not intended to provide a way for us to remove ourselves from the opportunities and challenges of life in the real world. Rather, it is to equip and empower us to make a difference there. Just as the believers in Rome found themselves at an important crossroads of social, economic, and political life, we too have each been placed in a unique position to influence our world for Christ. First, we must develop a clear understanding of what faith means to us—then we must let that understanding direct everything we do. What do you need to do in order to seize the opportunities God has given you to influence your world?

8 In what ways do we sometimes seem to be ashamed of the gospel? Why is this, and what should we do about it?

_____

_____

_____

_____

_____

R
RESPOND
to the message

9 What resources does your church have to make an impact on your community? How can the individual believer help?

_____

_____

_____

_____

_____

10 How have churches moved away from the fundamentals of faith? How can this be changed?

_____

_____

_____

_____

_____

11 In what situations do you have opportunities to influence others for Christ by the way you live? How effectively are you using these opportunities? What could you do to strengthen the impact of your witness?

_____

_____

_____

_____

_____

12 When you analyze the foundation of your own faith, where do you see that you need to be strengthened? Plan some steps you will take to review the basics of the Christian life.

RESOLVE
to take action

_____

_____

_____

_____

_____

_____

_____

A What is the gospel? Summarize its essential elements in terms of man's need, God's response, and the implications of this transaction for the life of faith.

MORE
for studying
other themes
in this section

B What is an apostle? How did Paul qualify?

C How was Paul prevented from visiting the church in Rome earlier? What does this teach about God's timing?

D Belonging to Christ is a good way of describing both the privileges and the responsibilities of being a Christian. List the most important aspects of each in terms of the life of faith.

E Describe the role and importance of prayer in relation to the spreading and nurturing of the gospel.

LESSON 2
WHATEVER BECAME OF SIN?
ROMANS 1:18–2:16

REFLECT
on your life

1 What are some activities that are widely accepted in our society now but were widely condemned just a few years ago?

_____

_____

_____

_____

2 How have your own standards changed over the years?

_____

_____

_____

_____

READ
the passage

Read Romans 1:18–2:16 and the following notes:

❏ 1:18 ❏ 1:21-32 ❏ 1:24-32 ❏ 1:25 ❏ 1:32 ❏ 2:1ff ❏ 2:4 ❏ 2:5-11
❏ 2:12-15

3 What does Paul's argument tell us about God?

_____

_____

_____

_____

4 What does it tell us about sin?

_____

_____

_____

5 What do we learn about human beings?

_____

_____

_____

_____

6 How would people in your congregation react if your pastor were to deliver such a confrontational message?

_____

_____

_____

7 What does Paul mean when he says that God "abandoned them" to their wickedness?

_____

_____

_____

REALIZE
the principle

8 Why does God hate sin so much? Why did Paul feel compelled to speak out so strongly on this issue to this audience?

_____

_____

_____

_____

God hates sin, and he wants us to hate it, too. Yet we live in a world where all types of immoral behavior are excused, explained away, or even defended on the basis of freedom and personal rights. Compromise is seen in every corner of our society and is praised as a virtue. But what about God's expectations? Surely the Creator's will is more important than the creature's desires. We must be willing to see our actions for what they are—sin—and we need to see clearly the consequences our sin may bring upon us and others. We will be held accountable for our actions. We must take bold action to remove sin's influence from our life and to stand for what is right and true whenever we encounter compromise.

9 What are some examples of compromise within our churches?

_____

_____

_____

_____

_____

RESPOND
to the message

10 Why are some Christians afraid to call certain actions sin?

_____

_____

_____

_____

_____

11 In what areas of your life have you compromised too far in your standards or behavior?

_____

_____

_____

_____

_____

12 How have God's standards been compromised in your church? in society? What can you do about this?

_____

_____

_____

_____

_____

13 How can we take a stand against sin without being vengeful or judgmental?

_____

_____

_____

_____

14 Choose an area of your life where you need to raise your standards. Ask yourself what is wrong with your current lifestyle or way of thinking. Write down what you think your actions should be. Ask God to give you the strength to make the necessary changes.

RESOLVE
to take action

_____

_____

_____

_____

15 Identify at least one person to whom you are willing to be accountable, and tell him or her the changes you think are required in your life. Ask your accountability partner to pray for you and to help you evaluate your progress.

_____

_____

A Who is the most godly person you know? How does he or she measure up to God's standards of perfection?

MORE
for studying
other themes
in this section

B Against what sin is God showing his anger? What choices are open to human beings? What choice do they make?

C What is your reaction to Paul's claim that creation itself tells about God and that people have "no excuse"?

D Why does Paul emphasize sexual immorality as an example of sin and its control over human beings? What's so serious about sexual sin?

E Why is idolatry still a problem for human beings in general? for Christians specifically?

F How do you reconcile the concept of a loving God with the idea that some people are abandoned to the consequences of their sin and will face eternal punishment? What can you do to save people from this terrible fate?

G How would you answer the question, "What happens to those people who never hear about Christ? Surely God wouldn't condemn them, would he?"

LESSON 3
NOT GUILTY!
ROMANS 2:17–3:31

REFLECT
on your life

1 At a time when you were accused of some wrongdoing, how did you feel? How did you try to deal with your feelings of guilt or shame?

_____

_____

_____

READ
the passage

Read Romans 2:17–3:31 and the following notes:

❏ 2:17ff   ❏ 2:21, 22   ❏ 2:21-27   ❏ 2:24   ❏ 3:1ff   ❏ 3:5-8   ❏ 3:10-18

❏ 3:19   ❏ 3:21-29   ❏ 3:23   ❏ 3:24   ❏ 3:27, 28   ❏ 3:28

2 Why do you think Paul addressed the Jews specifically at this point in the letter? Why wasn't his earlier condemnation enough to convince them of their sin?

_____

_____

_____

3 If there is not a single righteous person, what difference does it make that some are less sinful than others?

_____

_____

_____

4 What does it mean to be freely justified by God's grace?

_____

_____

_____

5 How does Paul explain faith and how it works? (See the chart entitled "What Is Faith?" near 1:26.) How does his concept differ from other common interpretations?

_____

_____

_____

_____

6 What are some advantages of growing up in a religious home? What are some disadvantages?

Advantages	*Disadvantages*
_____	_____
_____	_____
_____	_____
_____	_____

REALIZE
the principle

7 Paul presents the idea of the "true Jew" as a person whose heart is right with God. How does this idea apply to Christians?

_____

_____

_____

_____

Like the Jews to whom Paul was addressing his stinging criticism, Christians are often guilty of trying to please God by good works. Independence, self-sufficiency, hard-earned security, and personal control over one's life are cherished values today; it can be difficult to accept that there is no way to earn our way into heaven or to gain God's favor. We think that surely we deserve consideration for our efforts. We must accept, however, that even at our best we fall far short of God's perfect standard of righteous living. All our attempts to justify and excuse our actions count for nothing. The only way our sins can be forgiven is for us to accept God's gift. Through Christ, we are declared *not guilty*. We can never do enough either to deserve that gift or to repay God for his great mercy. We can only accept it.

8 Paul accused the Jews of relying on the law to save them. In what ways do Christians get caught up in the externals of religious practice and lose sight of the need for complete dependence on God's grace for salvation?

_____

_____

RESPOND
to the message

9 How have you tried to earn God's approval or repay him for forgiving your sins?

_____

_____

_____

_____

10 Evaluate these possible barriers to your accepting God's forgiveness by faith. On a scale of 1 to 5, with 1 being "not a barrier" and 5 being "a big barrier," circle the number you feel best describes each obstacle.

Suspicion of free offers (There must be a catch.)	1 2 3 4 5
Extreme guilt over past sins (I'm not sure I can be forgiven.)	1 2 3 4 5
Doing good in order to be worthy, or to repay God for his gift	1 2 3 4 5
Pride in being better than others	1 2 3 4 5
Taking God's grace for granted (A loving God has to forgive.)	1 2 3 4 5
Relying on externals (acts of service, rituals, church membership, correct doctrines, etc.)	1 2 3 4 5
Taking salvation for granted (I've been a Christian all my life, so I guess I'm safe.)	1 2 3 4 5
Justifying actions, making excuses, or blaming others (It's really not my fault.)	1 2 3 4 5
Minimizing personal sinfulness (What's wrong with doing this? Everybody does it.)	1 2 3 4 5
Not fearing God (I think the Bible exaggerates about God's anger and the severity of his judgment.)	1 2 3 4 5

11 How should the truth of being made right with God through faith affect Christians?

_____

_____

_____

12 What do your words and actions communicate to non-Christians about the nature of your faith?

_____

_____

_____

_____

13 What words or actions of yours might communicate a holier-than-thou attitude to nonbelievers? What reactions would you expect this to produce in them?

_____

_____

_____

_____

14 What difference should it make in your day-to-day actions to know that you cannot earn your way into heaven? Why isn't this like having a license to sin?

_____

_____

_____

15 Do you try to earn God's approval? Do you have a holier-than-thou attitude or make excuses for your mistakes? Do you rely on externals instead of on Christ's redemption? Do you take God's grace for granted and forget to thank him for his precious gift? How should you change your thoughts and actions today?

RESOLVE
to take action

_____

_____

_____

_____

A If keeping the law cannot save a Jew, what purpose does it serve? How does Christ's death affect the law? What is the role of the law in the context of grace?

MORE
for studying
other themes
in this section

B What are the modern parallels to the Jewish rite of circumcision? How might there be similar dangers involved?

C If Paul were writing Romans 2:17-24 to the Christian church today, how do you think he would change his message? How would his accusations apply to us?

D Think about each of the word pictures in Romans 3:11-18. What do these Old Testament quotations teach about our thoughts, direction, speech, and pursuits? What is the answer to this terrible picture?

E What ways of righteousness do people try? Why are these attempts futile?

LESSON 4
ABRAHAM, A MODEL OF FAITH
ROMANS 4:1-25

REFLECT
on your life

1 What does it mean to have faith in God?

_____

_____

_____

_____

_____

2 How does a person live by faith?

_____

_____

_____

_____

_____

READ
the passage

Read Romans 4:1-25 and the following notes:

❏ 4:5   ❏ 4:6-8   ❏ 4:10-12   ❏ 4:21   ❏ 4:25

3 What does Paul mean by the frequently used phrase "counted . . . as righteous"?

_____

_____

_____

_____

4 Abraham was an ideal example of a person of faith for both Jews and Gentiles. What characteristics of this great man help us identify with him?

_____

_____

_____

_____

_____

5 How did Abraham exemplify true faith?

_____

_____

_____

_____

Faith is not just believing that a certain series of events will come to pass—it is believing that God is faithful in fulfilling his promises. There is a subtle but important difference. The former way of thinking can cause us to keep taking things back into our own hands instead of relying on God to act in his way and in his time. Abraham experienced the consequences of trying to make everything work out by his own efforts. But he learned through his struggles how to rely totally on God. He learned the difference between hoping that situations will work out a certain way and trusting in God, who will fulfill his promises. This knowledge allowed Abraham to be used by God to bless all humankind. This is real, life-changing faith.

6 Today's rational person would say that having faith when there is no hope is simply foolishness. If you believe that God still does what is impossible, how might you try to persuade a skeptical person to be open to God's unexpected intervention?

_____

_____

_____

_____

7 Why is it so difficult for people today to live by faith? How do we take matters into our own hands and miss what God wants to do for us?

_____

_____

_____

_____

8 Someone might say, "If my salvation depends on faith, what happens when my faith isn't strong enough?" What would you say to reassure that person?

_____

_____

_____

_____

_____

_____

RESPOND
to the message

9 How is a life built on a foundation of faith better than one built on a foundation of just doing what is right?

_____

_____

_____

_____

_____

10 Abraham made mistakes, as have all of the heroes of the faith. What lessons can we learn from how these great men and women of God handled their moments of defeat?

_____

_____

_____

_____

_____

11 Imagine that the timeline below represents your life. Mark on it the periods or events that were your personal highs and lows in terms of living by faith. What lessons can you learn from these ups and downs?

_____

Birth   Present

_____

_____

_____

_____

12 What factors keep you from living more fully and consistently by faith?

_____

_____

_____

_____

_____

13 How would your life be different if you were living by faith? Choose at least one area of your life where you need to exercise more faith, and prayerfully turn it over to God. What does he want you to start (or perhaps stop) doing in this area?

RESOLVE
to take action

_____

_____

_____

_____

_____

A What other Old Testament characters might Paul have mentioned as heroes of the faith, and why?

MORE
for studying
other themes
in this section

B Paul describes Abraham as one whose faith never wavered, and yet Scripture tells us that he had his highs and lows. Recall the key events from Abraham's life, and draw a timeline to show the peaks and valleys of his faith experience.

C Paul talks about the promise God made to Abraham (Genesis 12), which included three parts—land, descendants, and blessing for all nations. How does this promise affect today's situation in the Middle East?

D How does God's promise to Abraham apply to Christians?

E Paul uses some interesting phrases to describe Abraham (for example, "father of all who believe," "father of many nations"). What does this suggest about the nature of God's family? What does being in God's family mean to you?

F Compare what Abraham believed about God with what we must believe about God if we are to be considered righteous.

G The truth for all ages is that people must not only believe _in_ God, they must also believe God. How would you explain to someone else exactly what faith in Jesus Christ means?

LESSON 5
FINDING PEACE WITH GOD
ROMANS 5:1—21

REFLECT
on your life

1 Where do you go and what do you do to experience peace and quiet? Why do we have to get away to have peace?

_____

_____

_____

_____

_____

2 How can we have peace even when life is not peaceful?

_____

_____

_____

_____

READ
the passage

Read Romans 5:1-21 and the following notes:

❏ 5:1   ❏ 5:3, 4   ❏ 5:6   ❏ 5:8   ❏ 5:9, 10   ❏ 5:11   ❏ 5:12   ❏ 5:13, 14
❏ 5:14   ❏ 5:15-19   ❏ 5:20

3 Paul tells us we have peace with God because of what Jesus Christ has done. How does this work? What is required of us in this process of reconciliation?

_____

_____

_____

_____

4 What is the difference between peace *with* God and the peace *of* God? How are they related?

_____

_____

_____

_____

_____

_____

5 This passage sets out three sources of joy for Christians: (1) rejoicing in sharing God's glory (verse 2); (2) rejoicing in problems and trials (verse 3); and (3) rejoicing in our relationship with God (verse 11). What does each of these mean?

_____

_____

_____

_____

_____

_____

6 How can life's problems help us to grow? How should we approach difficult times in order to experience the benefits God wants to bring through them?

REALIZE
the principle

_____

_____

_____

_____

_____

7 Why did God want to provide a way to reconcile people to himself?

_____

_____

_____

_____

_____

8 We were God's enemies—he could have destroyed us. What does the fact that God didn't do this say about him? What does it say about us?

_____

_____

_____

9 What was the essential difference between Adam and Jesus Christ? What does it mean to be a child of Adam? of Christ?

_____

_____

_____

_____

We are confronted with a clear choice. We can live as Adam's children and experience the troubling consequences of our identification with him, or we can live as God's children and rejoice in all that God gives us because of our identification with his Son, Jesus Christ. God wants us to have this kind of life, and that starts with making peace—being reconciled—with him. But we can't have peace with God unless we are willing to accept it on his terms. Does he expect us to live a perfect life or perform some regular act of service or religious duty to make him happy? No! He simply asks us to accept by faith that Jesus has once and for all done everything required to bring us to God, no matter what we've done to break that relationship. In our high-stress, modern world, where everything we want or need costs us something and where every relationship places demands on us, this is an offer we cannot afford to pass up.

RESPOND
to the message

10 If we are reconciled to God, what keeps us from enjoying the peace he promises?

_____

_____

_____

_____

11 Of the three sources of joy mentioned in question 5, which is most difficult for you to take hold of, and why?

_____

_____

_____

_____

12 Read the chart in chapter 5 entitled "What We Have as God's Children." Summarize the key differences between a life lived as a child of Adam and that lived as a child of God. Then describe the most important differences being God's child has made in your life.

_____

_____

_____

_____

13 After you have been reconciled to God, how can you demonstrate that peace in your life? What should people notice about you that is different from others who have not accepted God's gift of reconciliation?

_____

_____

_____

_____

14 Write down an area of your life where you are suffering right now and how God can use this experience to shape your character and mold you into the person he wants you to be. Write down ways in which you might be hindering him from helping you grow. Then commit yourself to removing those barriers in your thoughts or actions.

RESOLVE
to take action

_____

_____

_____

_____

_____

A What belongs to us because of Christ's blood? his death? his life? What must we do to receive these benefits?

MORE
for studying
other themes
in this section

B What does it mean that Christ came "at just the right time" (verse 6)? How should this affect our understanding of God's timing in other events in life?

C How can we be judged guilty for what Adam did?

D How did the giving of the law cause sin to increase? How does this cause God's kindness (grace) to increase even more? How might we distort this principle to satisfy our own desires?

LESSON 6
FREE TO CHOOSE LIFE
ROMANS 6:1-23

REFLECT
on your life

1 From where you are seated, what evidences of electrical power can you see?

_____

_____

_____

_____

_____

2 What would be the worst time for you to have a power outage?

_____

_____

_____

_____

READ
the passage

Read Romans 6:1-23 and the following notes:

☐ 6:1, 2 ☐ 6:1-4 ☐ 6:6, 7 ☐ 6:8, 9 ☐ 6:11 ☐ 6:14, 15 ☐ 6:16-18
☐ 6:17 ☐ 6:19-22 ☐ 6:23

3 What kinds of power does Paul discuss in this chapter?

_____

_____

_____

_____

4 Why did some people think they could go on sinning?

_____

_____

_____

_____

5 What does Paul mean when he challenges us to use our whole body as a tool to do what is right?

_____

REALIZE
the principle

_____

_____

_____

6 Where does personal choice fit into this?

_____

_____

_____

_____

_____

7 What should be different about someone who has fully become God's person?

_____

_____

_____

_____

_____

In this chapter we read about the truly miraculous power of the gospel—it sets us free to do what is right. Sin no longer controls us. It's not that Christians can't sin anymore, but that we are now free to choose between doing wrong and doing right. This Christ-bought freedom carries with it great responsibility. We must use our God-given power to make right choices, replacing our sinful thoughts and actions with righteous ones. This is what it means to choose life. Failure to do so means to remain enslaved to sin, and in the end we lose every-thing. But when we serve God, our rewards are abundant joy and eternal life. Give your life to the one who gave his life for you.

8 Study the chart at the end of chapter 6 entitled "What Has God Done about Sin?" Explain how each of these important principles applies to you.

_____

_____

_____

_____

_____

_____

_____

_____

_____

_____

R
RESPOND
to the message

9 If sin is no longer our master, why do we keep sinning?

_____

_____

_____

_____

10 What good is it to know that we are free from sin—how does that help us?

_____

_____

_____

_____

11 How is God shaping and molding you? How do you resist his work?

_____

_____

_____

_____

_____

12 Why should you give yourself totally to God? If you are willing to make such a commitment, what do you think God will demand of you?

_____

_____

_____

_____

_____

13 During this next week, when you feel the tug of sin, what will help you to choose to do what is right?

RESOLVE
to take action

_____

_____

_____

A How does baptism demonstrate and strengthen our identification with Jesus Christ as our Savior and Lord?

MORE
for studying
other themes
in this section

B How clear is the teaching of your church concerning the power God has given people to choose right over wrong? How can you help a fellow Christian who is struggling in this area?

C What could you tell someone who wants to know what is required to live a holy life?

D Look at the various roles you perform (spouse, parent, child, employee, church member, neighbor, etc.) and identify two or three situations in which you need to become more fully a man or woman of God. What will that require? How can you be a better servant in this area? Resolve to take action now.

LESSON 7
LOSING SIGHT OF THE VICTORY
ROMANS 7:1-25

R
REFLECT
on your life

1 When was a time you felt strongly tempted to do something you knew was wrong? Why was it so tempting?

_____

_____

_____

_____

_____

R
READ
the passage

Read Romans 7:1-25 and the following notes:

❐ 7:1ff ❐ 7:2-6 ❐ 7:4 ❐ 7:6 ❐ 7:9-11 ❐ 7:11, 12 ❐ 7:15 ❐ 7:23-25

2 This chapter begins by comparing life under the law with being married. Why is this comparison appropriate? How might Paul's audience have understood this and reacted?

_____

_____

_____

_____

_____

3 Why do God's laws arouse our sinful desires?

_____

_____

_____

_____

4 If the law causes so much difficulty for the believer, why didn't God eliminate it? What useful purpose does it serve?

_____

_____

_____

_____

_____

_____

5 What struggle is Paul describing?

_____

_____

_____

REALIZE
the principle

6 How can we be free from sin and yet continue to do wrong?

_____

_____

_____

_____

At first glance, this chapter presents a pretty gloomy picture of life as a daily struggle on the edge of defeat. Even Christians may feel powerless to defeat sin. _If faith isn't any more effective than that, what's the use of trying?_ we may think. Does victory come only after our earthly life is over? Most assuredly not! Paul's purpose is not to prepare us for our inevitable failure. Instead, he is challenging us not to deal with sin in our own strength. When we do so, we are bound to fail. We must always be ready to resist the desires of our old sinful nature. We can resist sin only through the power of Christ within us. We must always take sin seriously, even though we know we have eternal life through Christ. Take heart— the enemy has already been defeated!

7 What forces might cause strong spiritual leaders to stumble?

_____

_____

_____

_____

RESPOND
to the message

8 What makes us complacent about sin in our life?

_____

_____

_____

_____

9 One of the notes on 7:15 summarizes three lessons Paul shared. Restate these lessons in your own words. Which one is most important for you to emphasize in your life?

_____

_____

_____

_____

_____

_____

_____

10 How are you battling sin in your own strength? Identify some practical ways you can become more reliant on Christ in dealing with this struggle.

_____

_____

_____

_____

_____

RESOLVE
to take action

11 What temptations do you fight on your own? How can you depend more on God to help you fight temptation? How can other Christians help you?

_____

_____

_____

_____

_____

A Why is it dangerous to separate our sinful nature and our spiritual nature, blaming our sinful nature (or Satan) for our moral lapses?

B Why is it wrong to say, "Satan made me do it"?

C Many people speak as though the forces of good and evil are equal and opposite in our life. Why is this wrong?

D Why is it that we cannot live a holy life in our own strength any more than we can attain right standing before God by our own works?

MORE
for studying
other themes
in this section

L E S S O N   8
THE KEY TO CONFIDENT LIVING
ROMANS 8:1-39

R
REFLECT
on your life

1 Think of a time when you felt especially close to God—what was he doing in your life? Think of a time you felt distant from him—what caused the distance?

_____

_____

_____

_____

_____

R
READ
the passage

Read Romans 8:1-39 and the following notes:

❏ 8:1   ❏ 8:5, 6   ❏ 8:9   ❏ 8:14-17   ❏ 8:17   ❏ 8:24, 25   ❏ 8:26, 27
❏ 8:28   ❏ 8:29   ❏ 8:31-34   ❏ 8:35, 36   ❏ 8:35-39

2 Against what destructive forces were the Roman believers struggling? What might have caused them to feel separated from God's love?

_____

_____

_____

_____

_____

3 What are some ways the Holy Spirit empowers Christians to live victoriously?

_____

_____

_____

_____

4 With all the help God makes available, why do we still struggle?

_____

_____

_____

_____

REALIZE
the principle

5 What undermines our confidence in God's promises and keeps us from trusting fully in him?

_____

_____

_____

_____

6 What differences in one's outlook on life are there between someone living by the Spirit and someone living by the sinful nature?

_____

_____

_____

_____

Apart from Christ, we are doomed to failure and condemnation. But God did not leave us to this fate. He provided a way out, and he sent his Spirit to give us victory over sin. Our hope is not only in eternal life in the future—we can have a taste of that life right now. All we have to do is allow the Holy Spirit to guide us. We can know God's will; we can have God's peace; we can triumph over sin; we can profit from our trials; and we never can be lost to God's love. Be confident of God's consistent care now and an even better future with him in eternity. You can't lose! No matter what happens, God will give you the victory. So go wherever he leads!

7 The way Paul describes life in the Spirit, we have every reason to be confident, no matter what challenges we face. What evidence of this confidence should we see in the life of the believer?

RESPOND
to the message

_____

_____

_____

_____

_____

8 The Holy Spirit will express our deepest needs to God even when we don't know how to put them into words. How should this affect how we pray or what we pray for?

_____

_____

_____

_____

_____

9 How do we frustrate the Holy Spirit's work in our life?

_____

_____

_____

_____

_____

10 Recall a difficult experience that helped you grow significantly. How did God work everything out in your best interests?

_____

_____

_____

_____

_____

_____

RESOLVE
to take action

11 How do we balance relying on the Holy Spirit's power with relying on our own planning and resources? How do you need to change your thinking and acting?

_____

_____

_____

_____

_____

12 What can you do regularly to support the work of the Holy Spirit in your life?

_____

_____

_____

_____

_____

_____

A In 8:2-4, what reasons does Paul give for his confidence? How can you be confident in Christ?

MORE
for studying
other themes
in this section

B How do we know that we belong to Christ?

C Why did Paul describe our status as God's children in terms of adoption? What does this suggest concerning our relationship with God?

D At one point, Paul seems to say that God is going to give us whatever we ask for. How might we abuse this promise? How can this promise help us?

E How do we share in Christ's sufferings? What impact should this have on our life?

F What do we have to look forward to with the coming of the new heaven and the new earth that God has promised?

G What does Paul mean by the words "God knew his people in advance" (verse 29)? How can we explain this in a way that is consistent with God's love, mercy, and justice? What difference does it make in your life to know that you have been chosen by God?

H How do angels and demons operate in the world today?

LESSON 9
SEARCHING FOR GOD AND MISSING JESUS
ROMANS 9:1–11:36

R
REFLECT
on your life

1 Before you became a Christian, where did you look for meaning and purpose in life? What kept you from turning to Christ sooner?

_____

_____

_____

_____

R
READ
the passage

Read Romans 9:1–11:36 and the following notes:

❏ 9:1-3 ❏ 9:21 ❏ 9:31-33 ❏ 9:32 ❏ 10:3-5 ❏ 10:8-12 ❏ 10:14

❏ 10:15 ❏ 10:18-20 ❏ 11:2 ❏ 11:6 ❏ 11:16-24 ❏ 11:26

2 Why is Paul so upset about the Jews' lack of response to the gospel?

_____

_____

_____

_____

3 Paul seems to be searching for possible explanations for this very troubling problem. What are some of the solutions he explores?

_____

_____

_____

_____

4 How would these solutions also apply to Gentiles?

_____

_____

_____

_____

5 If God has not given up on his chosen people, what more can he do to reach them in this day and age?

_____

_____

_____

_____

6 Why do you think God has been so patient in dealing with the Jews' stubborn resistance to the gospel?

_____

REALIZE
the principle

_____

_____

_____

7 Why do people look for answers to life's questions in so many different places?

_____

_____

_____

_____

8 Even when the gospel is clearly presented, many reject its saving message. How can we encourage them to accept Christ?

_____

_____

_____

_____

God's promises are forever. This is Paul's consolation for the unresponsiveness of the Jews. One day all those who belong to the true Israel will acknowledge Christ as the promised Messiah. In the meantime, God has provided wonderful rewards for the rest of his children. All who believe can have eternal life through his Son. But we must never allow our privileges as believers to make us proud or boastful—we had nothing to do with our salvation. We were saved only through God's grace, by an act of his love. And that love was first promised to those he raised up to be his holy nation. God will never forsake them, just as he will never forsake us. Rather than sitting back and basking in the warm glow of our relationship with God, we should be searching diligently for ways to help others find the only true source of everlasting life.

R
RESPOND
to the message

9 In what ways might those who have grown up in Christian families rely too heavily on their Christian heritage?

_____

_____

_____

_____

10 What are some major sidetracks and pitfalls that keep people from discovering Jesus today? How can we expose the futility of following these paths?

_____

_____

_____

_____

_____

11 In what ways are you still trying to earn God's approval all over again?

_____

_____

_____

_____

12 What people do you feel the strongest desire to reach with the gospel?

_____

_____

_____

_____

13 What fears keep us from sharing the gospel with others?

_____

_____

_____

_____

_____

14 Whom do you know who is currently seeking meaning, purpose, and direction in life? Try to understand his or her greatest felt needs. Find ways both to tell
this person and to show him or her how Christ can meet one's deepest needs.
Write down what you might say.

RESOLVE
to take action

_____

_____

_____

_____

_____

_____

_____

A What great spiritual heritage do Jews have? Describe your spiritual heritage.

MORE
for studying
other themes
in this section

B How do you deal with Paul's statements concerning God's decision to save
some and not others, to harden the hearts and to shut the eyes and the ears of
some?

C What made it so easy for the Jews to stumble over Jesus?

D What was Paul implying through the use of the grafting image? What possible
wrong impressions, particularly among Gentile believers, was he attempting to
correct?

E How can righteousness be attained? Who succeeds in being righteous? Who
fails? Why?

LESSON 10
BECOMING A LIVING SACRIFICE
ROMANS 12:1-21

REFLECT
on your life

1 When have you really had to sacrifice for something? What did you give up? What made you willing to invest so much of yourself to achieve that goal?

_____

_____

_____

_____

_____

_____

READ
the passage

Read Romans 12:1-21 and the following notes:

❐ 12:1   ❐ 12:1, 2   ❐ 12:2   ❐ 12:3   ❐ 12:6   ❐ 12:6-8   ❐ 12:9-10   ❐ 12:10
❐ 12:13   ❐ 12:17-21   ❐ 12:19-21

2 What sacrifice is Paul talking about?

_____

_____

_____

_____

3 What does Paul mean when he writes, "Be honest in your evaluation of yourselves" (verse 3)?

_____

_____

_____

_____

4 How can good overcome evil?

_____

_____

_____

_____

5 How does the world define success? How are we pressured to conform
to these standards?

REALIZE
the principle

_____

_____

_____

_____

_____

6 What can we do to resist the pressures of the world? What does it mean
to refuse to conform?

_____

_____

_____

_____

7 What does it mean to let God change the way you think? How can this
happen?

_____

_____

_____

_____

8 How can you tell the difference between sincere and phony love? What is
more common today and why?

_____

_____

_____

_____

For Christians, sacrifice does not involve killing an animal on an altar—it is willingly surrendering ourselves to the will of God. And we don't do this because of what we will gain or even because we know it is right. We do it out of gratitude for what God has already done for us through Jesus Christ. This living sacrifice involves the body, mind, and will. There can be no holding back. Living sacrificially can be difficult when life is easy and comfortable, and where success is defined by the world in terms of "more is better." When we have so much, we lose sight of the fundamental importance of serving God through serving others. We focus on our own needs and defend our rights. As a result, we don't show others the kind of love the Lord has shown to us. We need to get our thinking straight if we are going to build God's Kingdom together.

R
RESPOND
to the message

9 What keeps us from giving our body to God for service? our mind? our will? Why is it so difficult for us to sacrifice?

_____

_____

_____

_____

_____

_____

_____

10 Why can forgiveness be hard to give and to receive? Where do you need to become more forgiving? Where do you need to be forgiven?

_____

_____

_____

_____

_____

11 If someone filmed the past week of your life, what sacrifices would they have recorded? What evidence of conforming to the world's standards would they see? what acts of selflessness? what evidence of selfishness?

_____

_____

_____

_____

_____

12 Verses 9-19 contain a number of attributes that we can struggle with as we try to love others. Evaluate yourself by circling the number that best represents how you are doing with each attribute.

RESOLVE
to take action

		Not a problem		Somewhat of a problem		Serious problem
12:9	sincerity	1	2	3	4	5
12:10	love	1	2	3	4	5
12:11	enthusiasm	1	2	3	4	5
12:12	patience	1	2	3	4	5
12:13	sharing	1	2	3	4	5
12:13	hospitality	1	2	3	4	5
12:15	empathy	1	2	3	4	5
12:16	harmony	1	2	3	4	5
12:16	pride	1	2	3	4	5
12:19	revenge	1	2	3	4	5

Which ones do you struggle with the most? What could you do about these?

_____

_____

_____

_____

_____

_____

13 Review the trouble spots in the chart above. What are you prepared to do this week to demonstrate your love for others in these areas?

_____

_____

A How did Paul know what issues the church in Rome struggled with if he had never been there?

MORE
for studying
other themes
in this section

B In Romans 12:3, what does Paul suggest concerning the use of our mind?

C List the spiritual gifts in Romans 12:6-8. Define each in concrete, practical terms.

D What might help you and other believers understand Paul's teachings more fully and apply them more effectively? How can you identify your spiritual gifts?

LESSON 11
CONTROLLED BY LOVE
ROMANS 13:1-14

R REFLECT on your life

1 If you only had six months to live, what changes would you make in your life? How about six weeks? six days?

_____

_____

_____

_____

_____

_____

R READ the passage

Read Romans 13:1-14 and the following notes:

❑ 13:1   ❑ 13:1ff   ❑ 13:3, 4   ❑ 13:8   ❑ 13:9   ❑ 13:10   ❑ 13:12-14   ❑ 13:14

2 How did the Roman government treat Jews and Christians?

_____

_____

_____

_____

3 What are some of the characteristics of good government that are outlined in the first part of the chapter?

_____

_____

_____

_____

4 Where else does the Bible talk about the connection between loving others and fulfilling the law?

_____

_____

_____

_____

5 Why do you think Paul closed this chapter with such a note of urgency?

_____

_____

6 What does it mean to give respect and honor to someone in authority?

_____

_____

_____

REALIZE
the principle

7 How is obeying authority a matter of conscience or principle, rather than simply one of avoiding punishment?

_____

_____

_____

_____

8 In what way is love a proof of faith?

_____

_____

_____

_____

This chapter discusses obeying authority, loving others as fulfillment of the law, and living with anticipation and a sense of urgency. As Christians, it is important that everything we say and do communicates clearly that we love God and others. This message can so easily be compromised by refusing to submit to authority, being preoccupied with our own selfish needs, or not being disciplined in doing what is right. All of this can distract us from our purpose, drain us of our resources, and dilute our witness. Our walk and our talk must agree or we won't be able to influence our world for Christ. The world desperately needs people who are willing to allow their actions to be motivated by concern for others and not by selfish desires. What do others see in you?

9 How do we compromise our Christian witness in the way we obey authority? in the way we relate to others?

_____

_____

_____

_____

_____

_____

_____

RESPOND
to the message

10 How should you regard those currently in authority over you? What actions or attitudes of leaders or officials make it more difficult for you to obey them?

_____

_____

_____

_____

_____

11 What does this passage suggest about the Christian's attitude toward civil disobedience? What can we do to take a stand for what we believe is right?

_____

_____

_____

_____

_____

12 How does Paul's principle of obedience apply when people find themselves under the authority of a corrupt government?

_____

_____

_____

_____

13 Who are some of the people in authority over you at home, school, work, church, and in the government?

_____

_____

_____

_____

_____

14 Think of a situation where you have a poor attitude toward someone in authority over you. What needs to change in your thoughts and actions to handle this situation more respectfully and lovingly? How might you start working on this today?

RESOLVE
to take action

_____

_____

_____

_____

_____

_____

A What conditions in the Roman Empire greatly assisted the spread of the gospel? What events from Paul's own life might explain his high view of the Roman authorities?

MORE
for studying
other themes
in this section

B What reason does Paul give for submitting to civil authorities?

C How does this passage relate to the sovereignty of God? to faith and hope?

D In what instances did Jesus or his followers disobey the political authorities? How might we interpret such acts?

E When and why should civil rulers be feared?

F What do you think should be the responsible Christian attitude toward the separation of church and state? What implications does this have for our participation in politics and government?

G What different interpretations might we give for Paul's statement that "our salvation is nearer now than when we first believed" (verse 11)?

H How might you live differently if you knew the Lord's return was near? What can you do to implement some of these changes now?

LESSON 12
LIVING FOR EACH OTHER
ROMANS 14:1–15:13

1 When have you been judged unfairly? How did you feel? How did this affect your relationship with the person who judged you?

_____

_____

_____

_____

_____

2 Think of a time when you hurt someone by something you did or said. What were the immediate and long-term results?

_____

_____

_____

_____

_____

Read Romans 14:1–15:13 and the following notes:

❐ 14:1   ❐ 14:1ff   ❐ 14:2   ❐ 14:10-12   ❐ 14:13   ❐ 14:13ff   ❐ 14:20, 21   ❐ 14:23

3 Why was it important for the Roman Christians to stay out of arguments over certain matters of faith and practice?

_____

_____

_____

_____

4 What were, and are, the essentials of faith and practice about which there should be no compromise?

_____

_____

_____

_____

_____

5 What does it mean to be weak in faith?

_____

_____

_____

_____

6 List some issues that cause division in the church at large. Do these issues trouble your own church as well? How might these be handled better?

_____

_____

_____

_____

_____

REALIZE
the principle

7 What does the apostle Paul mean when he asks, "Who are you to condemn someone else's servants" (14:4)? How should this affect our thoughts and speech about others?

_____

_____

_____

_____

8 Why is the stronger believer responsible to change his or her behavior so as not to offend the weaker brother or sister?

_____

_____

_____

9 Christian fellowship and biblical truth are both important sources of hope and encouragement for believers. What is the unique role of each, and why are both necessary?

_____

_____

_____

_____

_____

Dependent, independent, interdependent—how would you describe your experience in relation to other Christians? When we are weak, we are dependent, relying on others and needing their encouragement. But when we are strong, we tend to live on our own, feeling as though we need no one. Paul challenges us to grow beyond thinking, "I can do it myself." Instead, we should be interdependent, living for each other. Interdependence may be demonstrated in a variety of ways. Handling our differences in a way that strengthens each other is one. Meeting the needs of each other through material gifts, spiritual encouragement, and prayer are others. When we live for each other, we become more than fellow believers; we become a family. And that is what God desires us to be.

RESPOND
to the message

10 What steps can a church take to work through differences of opinion?

_____

_____

_____

_____

_____

11 Why is it difficult to suppress our own point of view in order to help those who are weaker in the faith?

_____

_____

_____

12 What is the difference between living for the good of others and living to please others?

_____

_____

_____

13 What should we try to achieve in our relationships with other Christians?

_____

_____

_____

14 How does mutual caring in relationships give us hope and peace?

_____

_____

_____

_____

15 How can you be more sensitive in your personal relationships?

_____

_____

_____

_____

_____

16 What are some areas in which you have Christian freedom but need to exercise more restraint? What are you prepared to sacrifice for the sake of others?

RESOLVE
to take action

_____

_____

_____

_____

_____

A What do you think will happen when we stand before God's judgment seat? How will the experience of believers and nonbelievers differ?

MORE
for studying
other themes
in this section

B How should Christians handle situations where opinions differ about what conduct is right?

LESSON 13
PARTNERS IN THE GOSPEL
ROMANS 15:14–16:27

REFLECT
on your life

1 Make a list of ways you can support someone. How have you been supported in each of those ways?

_____

_____

_____

_____

_____

READ
the passage

Read Romans 15:14–16:27 and the following notes:

❐ 15:22   ❐ 15:23, 24   ❐ 15:30   ❐ 16:1, 2   ❐ 16:3   ❐ 16:5ff   ❐ 16:7

❐ 16:17-20   ❐ 16:21   ❐ 16:25-27

2 How could Paul be so sure the Roman Christians were capable of teaching each other in the faith?

_____

_____

_____

_____

_____

3 What do these concluding verses of chapter 15 communicate about Paul's mission and motivation for ministry?

_____

_____

_____

_____

4 Why would Paul be concerned that his service to the Jerusalem church might not prove acceptable?

_____

_____

_____

_____

_____

5 How did Paul come to know so many of the Roman believers? What does this say about the spread of the gospel throughout Asia during those early years of the church?

_____

_____

_____

_____

_____

_____

6 This passage suggests it is all right to take pride in what God has done through us. What are some healthy and unhealthy ways of handling this issue?

REALIZE
the principle

_____

_____

_____

_____

_____

_____

7 Most of the church's outstanding leaders were highly motivated. How do people develop this high level of commitment?

_____

_____

_____

_____

_____

_____

8 What practical ways to support others are found in this passage?

_____

_____

_____

_____

_____

_____

In this section we see how fellowship makes a difference. The relationships we read about were not just social acquaintances. They were deep commitments to one another that came from struggling together to achieve a common goal. When you have prayed, worked, laughed, and cried with someone, the friendship will not be weakened by time or distance. When you have had a part in another's growth, you will always have a part in the fruit of that person's service. And in difficult times, you turn to those whose love has been demonstrated and tested. That's what our true partners in the gospel are like. Look around—who else is working faithfully alongside you?

R
RESPOND
to the message

9 What has Christ accomplished through you? How have others encouraged you as you have served the Lord?

_____

_____

_____

_____

_____

_____

10 What changes would you like to see in the type or amount of support you receive from others in your church?

_____

_____

_____

_____

_____

11 How could you be more supportive of others?

_____

_____

_____

_____

12 Think of a person you know who needs extra support right now to over-come a struggle or accomplish a difficult task. How can you help that person this week?

_____

_____

_____

_____

_____

RESOLVE
to take action

A What does Scripture seem to indicate about Paul's activity after he wrote this letter?

B What is the secret of the gospel, and how was it hidden from the beginning of time (16:25)?

MORE
for studying
other themes
in this section

Take Your Bible Study
to the Next Level

The **Life Application Study Bible** helps you apply truths in God's Word to everyday life. It's packed with nearly 10,000 notes and features that make it today's #1–selling study Bible.

Life Application Notes: Thousands of Life Application notes help explain God's Word and challenge you to apply the truth of Scripture to your life.

Personality Profiles: You can benefit from the life experiences of over a hundred Bible figures.

Book Introductions: These provide vital statistics, an overview, and a timeline to help you quickly understand the message of each book.

Maps: Over 200 maps next to the Bible text highlight important Bible places and events.

Christian Worker's Resource: Enhance your ministry effectiveness with this practical supplement.

Charts: Over 260 charts help explain difficult concepts and relationships.

Harmony of the Gospels: Using a unique numbering system, the events from all four Gospels are harmonized into one chronological account.

Daily Reading Plan: This reading plan is your guide to reading through the entire Bible in one unforgettable year.

Topical Index: A master index provides instant access to Bible passages and features that address the topics on your mind.

Dictionary/Concordance: With entries for many of the important words in the Bible, this is an excellent starting place for studying the Bible text.

Available in the New Living Translation, New International Version, King James Version, and New King James Version. Take an interactive tour of the *Life Application Study Bible* at
www.NewLivingTranslation.com/LASB